THE BOOK OF STAN

Observations of Life by the
Alter Ego of Dan Bailey

Dan Bailey

Copyright © 2023 Dan Bailey

All rights reserved

No part of this book may be reproduced, or stored in a retrieval system, or transmitted in any form or by any means, electronic, mechanical, photocopying, recording, or otherwise, without express written permission of the publisher.

ISBN-13: 979-8-9887773-1-1

Printed in the United States of America

Dedication

To all the textbooks, teachers, books, radio shows, newspapers, nature shows, documentaries, podcasts, websites, and conversations with friends, Romans, and countrymen. I lent you my ear and I am better for it.

NOTE ABOUT CONTENTS

Some of the stories and essays that follow were posted years ago on a website that I set up for friends to visit. Because of that, those stories may be considered previously published, though they have been updated for this publication. Stories that were on the site are marked with an asterisk next to the title.

CONTENTS

Title Page
Copyright
Dedication
Note about Contents
IMPORTANT NOTICES — 1
This page — 2
Welcome — 3
Who Is Stan? — 5
Flying Companions* — 7
Section I: The Irwinian Theorem — 11
Zebra Stripes — 13
Sensus Communis — 17
Sixth Sense — 24
The Formula — 30
Section II: Relationships — 35
Care* — 36
Wanted: A good man with a chainsaw* — 38
Pros or Cons — 40
Dancing As One — 42
Balance — 44
Yin and Yang — 49

Dating	51
Just A Little Nervous	56
Divorce	60
Give and Take	66
Computer Dating Ad Terminology*	73
Computer Ad Reply	78
An Independent Woman	80
S.O.U.P.	81
Overload	84
Why Do Men? Part I	87
Why Do Men? Part II	89
Good Question	91
One	94
Section III: Humor	95
The Bathroom*	96
Aisle 17	99
You can't be talking about me!	102
The FSRA	106
Gizmos*	109
A 9 or a 2*	111
Hair Loss*	115
Viva la Resolucionne'	117
New Year's 2006	119
Politics and Religion	121
The Grand Conspiracy*	122
The Lotion Bottle	124
The Verge of Sanity	127
Therapy*	130

Section IV: Miscellany and Thoughts	133
Simplified	134
Birthdays*	137
Middle Age Sane	140
A Long Walk in the Woods	143
Drum Beaters	145
International Diplomacy	148
Dad	150
Did I discover myself?	153
Funny	156
Spoiler Or Partner	158
FUTILITY	161
Objectivity and Perspective	162
Something I thought of while I was taking a shower	166
photo-sophic	169
Self-Centered or Selfish	170
The Big Picture	172
Trite	174
The Butterfly Effect	176
The Butterfly Factor	178
The Leaf	180
The Santa Claus Syndrome*	182
Theater	186
Section V: And Then…	187
A Brief History	188
One-Liners	198
The Last Word	206

IMPORTANT NOTICES

This book is optimized for and is best viewed with... a shot of tequila.

No Artificial Intelligence was used in the production of this book. After reading, you may have your doubts as to whether any Real Intelligence was used, as well.

Any similarity between the characters or entities portrayed herein and any person or entity, living or dead, just goes to show that I am not the only one this screwed up.

No animals were harmed during the production of the content of this site. The post-production party... now that's a different story.

It is possible that you will achieve greater financial success after becoming a Friend of Stan. If this were to take place, don't forget, Stan doesn't need your money, but I do.

THIS PAGE

**was intentionally
left blank.**

I am not sure what my intentions were…
But I did it on purpose.

WELCOME

What follows are the Words of Stan. He can be a bit sarcastic, and that will often come across in his humor. He also has a reflective side that reveals itself in some of the stories. Take some time to get to know him and you may be surprised.

The Irwinian Theorem and Relationships sections, in my humble opinion, contain some sharp observations about how people interact and should be read by anyone single and dating. It should be read by everyone, but I know some of you are busy. If you are married and dating... well, I got nothing. You are probably too tired to read anyway.

This book was finished in 2023, but many of the essays and short stories within have been written here and there since the late 1990s. Some of the stories were posted on the www.bookofstan.com website that I put up so friends could read them, though the site wasn't visited very often (insert sad face). I mention that so you know that a few stories have been "previously published," which I take to mean, in the publishing world at least, that they aren't virgins. Stories that were posted on the website are noted with an asterisk in the index. Not that the stories won't be new to you, they just have more experience than some of the other stories.

About those older stories. I have revisited each and edited and updated them. Oxford commas and so forth. For some, my twenty-year older self was pleased with my younger self. Others, well... a touch more work was in order. Apparently, I was too busy doing research back then.

So you know, neither Stan nor I have any degrees that would add to the weight of the words herein. However, you should know what you are good at, and I am good at observing people and knowing what they are feeling. In addition to my own pursuit of the fairer sex, I have been able to talk to hundreds of people and the conversation often gets to dating. With each, it seemed we performed a post-mortem about their relationships and what drives them. And what drives them away.

Besides all that, I am one of those people who sees the humor in everyday life, and a lot of those things end up getting written - well, typed - down. Some of this stuff still makes me laugh, so, hopefully, you will get a grin or two.

I hope you enjoy the read. I welcome any comment or suggestion and will promptly pass it on to Stan.

Regards, Dan

PS - if your suggestion involves where Stan can put his stories... it has already been made.

WHO IS STAN?

Good question... and one I have been asked many times. I generally say that he is my "alter ego" or my "evil twin." His origins are based in mistaken enunciation (no - that is not part of the Catholic confirmation process). Stan is actually a name I picked up a few years ago at the office.

When I answered the phone, I apparently would talk maybe a bit too fast, which went very well with talking too much. When I said, "this is Dan", the "isDan" ran together and some people understood me to be saying "this is Stan." When some of the customers asked for Stan, we all just shook our heads. It was somewhat perplexing until we figured out it was me, and then it was just funny.

I worked on my articulation, but phones have a tendency to obscure a few letters and "s" is one of them. The perpetuation of Stan was inevitable. If I was not going to be able to get rid of Stan, I figured I would make the best of him. Any mistake I made was blamed on Stan. Memorable phrases like "Stan has left the building" and "Stan? Stan's not here man" became office standards. Stan even made his way into everyday office talk with grammatical variances such as "Stan this into the computer", "Oh no. We've been Stanned !!", and the ever popular, "We are totally Stanned."

In general, Stan is the guy that shows up around the time the second glass of wine is down. Vino Veritas! He tends to talk a bit too much and can give away too many of my secrets. He also gets into my personal business too often, causing me to occasionally say or do the wrong thing, usually when I am dating someone. I would never personally be scared of closeness or intimacy... but Stan, he can really be a tight-ass sometimes.

While Stan was in his infancy, an Atlanta newspaper ran a radio spot in which a guy named, interestingly, Dan had an evil alter ego named, interestingly, Stan. I still need to find out if I should be getting royalties on that deal. Public notoriety did seal the process though and Stan has been my faithful - or fateful - sidekick ever since.

Gotta go now...

"Stan, where's my black shoes? You wore them last!"

FLYING COMPANIONS*

A while back, I went to Philadelphia on business. It was just a quick trip to meet a vendor, so I flew up one morning and was coming back on the 4:10 flight that afternoon. After the meeting, I dropped my rental and got the bus to the terminal. On the bus were other people also catching a flight back to Atlanta. They told me that the airline had changed airplanes and they were calling passengers to ask them to wait for the next flight.

This was not good. I had set this up and timed it so I could get back home at a decent hour, and I did not want to hear about a problem with the plane. Not that it was a rough trip, but whenever you fly somewhere and back on the same day, you want it to go smoothly. Thankfully, I was handed my boarding pass at the gate without delay. Great! No problems.

37F... Wait a minute! I had an aisle seat, and they gave me a window. Well, it could be worse. At least I was on the flight. I got on the plane and headed back. 34, 35, 36... Oh, no!! Bad news and good news. Which do you want first? Ok - the good news. 36E & F were taken, and the aisle seat was open. Yay!! Now the bad news. E & F were occupied by a seven-year-old and his ten-year-old brother, and - insert scary movie sound - they were flying alone.

"Oh, don't worry, Mrs. Johnson. The airline will ensure that your children are well looked after by someone on the flight" By ME.

Uh Oh!! I had done this before, and it can get pretty ugly.

I sat down, and it started.

"Hi! We are brothers. That's why we have the same type of shirt. Have you flown before?"

"Yes."

"We haven't. What's it like? Is it fun? Why aren't we moving?"

"We are still at the gate... it will be a few minutes."

All the adults in the surrounding seats gave me that look that said, "Keep your chin up... but, no, I won't swap seats with you." All were happy they were not in my seat and were looking to me to see how I would handle this. Even the flight attendants wouldn't make direct eye contact with me. Lamar, the younger of the two, was in the seat next to me (Lamont had the window), and his grandmother had packed enough goodies in his backpack to feed, well - you know how grandmothers are. Slim Jims, Gummy Life Savers, chewing gum, etc., and Lamar was eating with abandon. I casually looked through the "seat pocket located on the back of the seat in front of me" to get the paper bag ready. I wasn't being pessimistic. I just wanted to be prepared.

"What's your name?"

"Dan"

"When do we leave? What are those men doing out there? Can I have something to drink?"

"Attendant, bring me a drink."

Wouldn't you know it? The guy across the aisle was an IT professional. I could use this quality time to see if I could sell him some computer equipment. It wasn't gonna happen.

Then Lamar opened his bag and pulled out a notebook and pencil. He wrote at the top, "Our First Plane Ride." He then started writing the body of his report. I was happy. It was the first time he had quit eating since I sat down. I looked back down at what he was writing. "On the plane, Lamont and I met a very nice man named Dan." Ok - I was doomed. Then, to add to the guilt of my misgivings, he turned with a big smile and said, "Lamont and I were scared until you got here."

With an exhaled breath, I resigned myself to my job as In Loco Parentis, parent of the moment. I had to tell myself that I could easily stand the inconvenience since Lamar and Lamont would forever be affected by this first flying experience, and I would only be affected for two hours.

I answered their questions. Well, most of them. I helped them get what they needed from the flight attendant. I told them where the sun was. I got my drinks for free.

I got up to stretch my legs and turned around to see the three ladies in the seats behind me smiling. I told them the show would be over soon. One said they were giving me a "sitting, standing ovation" for being so nice to the boys. Hey, where are you now when I need a date?

I got a couple of stares from a guy in the next row that must have thought I was supposed to keep the boys quiet so he could relax. So, I encouraged them to talk more.

The rest of the flight went fine, and all in all, it wasn't so bad. The computer guy even joined in talking with the kids, and we got to know each other a little. The lady behind me had complimented me, and Lamar was enshrining me in a school report. When we landed, Lamar and Lamont had already made it to their mom by the time I was off the jetway. I stopped and put my hand on her shoulder. "Your children were very well-behaved on the plane." Lamar and Lamont were beaming. Throughout the terminal, train, and baggage pickup areas, every time I made eye contact, they waved and smiled.

I must have told this story four times the next day (probably many more). Whenever I related the part about what Lamar wrote, my co-workers smiled, knowing I would be an easy pushover for the kids.

I was wrong on the plane when I thought I would only be affected for two hours.

Lamar. Lamont. Thanks for the opportunity to sit with you.

SECTION I: THE IRWINIAN THEOREM

Pythagoras and Euclid had their geometry; Schrödinger had his cat (in a box); and Julia Child had her mastery of French cooking. They, and a long list of others with their theorems, principles, and processes related to their disciplines, are all safe from me. The heavy science guys are especially safe since all my advanced math classes went away when I figured out that I only needed to go to two classes a day to graduate high school. This resulted in my being a better cook than a mathematician, albeit without hollandaise sauce.

That said, any well-thought-out religion, writing, following, scientific theory, or TV diet guru has a foundation, a basic set of principles or guidelines, and a framework of truths and axioms that one can always refer to for reinforcement and explanation of the essence of that particular regimen.

I don't have that.

But, I do have what I call the Irwinian Theorem.

Note: My middle name is Irwin, so I wanted to get some mileage out of a middle name that is best referred to with an initial.

Simply put, the foundation of the Irwinian Theorem is that all people, regardless of circumstance, are the sum total of all their physical and mental experiences. That where you are, who you are, and what you create or do is a direct result of all the sensory input and mental cogitation, both normal and abnormal, that you have experienced, built upon your original being at birth, born of your parents' genetic combination.

I break the Theorem into four major components, in which I explain my take on how we get from where we start to where we are. The final portion, The Formula, boils it all down and presents a simple yet instructive way to look at our interactions with others.

Zebra Stripes

Sensus Communis

The Sixth Sense

The Formula

ZEBRA STRIPES

One day I was hanging out at the pool with friends. When we gathered like this, the conversation could go just about anywhere and quite often did. We were all single, and it was often the case that the conversation would turn toward relationships or lack thereof. One of the girls, we'll call her Betty, said, "What I don't understand is that every time I walk into a room with a bunch of men in it, within five minutes, I am talking to the two that just got out of prison."

The takeaway was that Betty, in her way, was saying what so many people say about how they get into and out of relationships. Something invariably attracts them to people of a set personality type while, conversely, drawing that type of person to them. Like everyone else to whom they have had a strong attraction.

Upon meeting someone new, there may appear to be a lot of difference between this one and the people they were attracted to in the past. Maybe the positive qualities, such as niceness, are more substantial with this one, or perhaps the "bad boy" side of the next is more alluring. But, as time goes on, they prove to be "just like" the last one and the one before and the one before. You've probably heard your single friends say, "I thought he was different than all the others." Or "I felt so comfortable with her. It was as if I had known her for years."

Or, maybe you remember saying that yourself. "It was love at first sight." "I knew it when she walked into the room." "When I first saw him standing there, I knew." All lines from movies and, like so many lines from movies, also lines from life.

Several years ago, I watched a nature show about the various animals on the plains of the Serengeti or somewhere in Africa. They did a segment on the zebra herds that I found interesting. Not that you would notice when looking at the herd, but every zebra has a different stripe pattern, like fingerprints. If you look at the herd on TV, there's no way you can see the difference between one zebra and another. Someone at some time must have stared long enough to see it.

Also, it seems we're not the only ones easily confused. The program related that when a zebra colt is born, it doesn't have a mechanism to recognize its mother. Like a horse, the zebra colt is born eyes open and can immediately stand up and move about. To keep the newborn from getting lost amid the visual noise of all the stripes around them, the mother must ensure that the colt can recognize her. To this end, the zebra mother positions herself in front of the colt and does not allow the colt to see any of the other zebras but her. If the colt turns to the right, the mother moves to the right, and so on. This bonding process goes on for the first 24 hours of life, during which the colt has his mother's unique stripe pattern firmly fixed in his memory. After this, the colt can recognize his mother from across the plain, mixed with the rest of the herd with their seemingly similar stripes.

Because we are first animals and then humans, I place a lot of value in the ability to learn from the way animals act. As I contemplated how this pattern imprinting affected the zebra colt, I couldn't help but think about how this equates to human behavior. We know the same thing happens to human babies. Most of us spend that crucial first day or two in the arms of or in the presence of our mother, primarily and, secondarily, our father. We are cared for; we are nurtured; we bond. These two people are all that we need in our life and, for the most part, all that exists.

The bonding is undeniable, as is the imprinting.

But what is this "imprinting?" It is more than just the ability to recognize one's parents in a crowded mall. Parents may feel great awe for their baby, but they are still human and are two people with their character traits, full of flaws, strengths, fears, and elations. A baby can't reason. A baby doesn't have the past to draw from or a concept that the future could be different. They can only perceive and sense what is. Their parents are the imprint on their lives, and the imprinting continues through infancy, becoming an invisible hand that influences them as adults.

As a result of this imprinting, we are bound to a subconscious recognition of the type of men and women we find comfort in and to whom we are attracted. Because it occurs subconsciously, it is also unavoidable and uncontrollable. For example, let's say there are ten basic types of imprinting, numbered, as you may have guessed, one through ten. This isn't a ranking system, so value and order don't matter. Say you are a two and always end up with an eight - a little with sevens and occasionally nines, but always somewhere in the same area. And when you are with a seven, if a good eight comes onto the scene, you are subject to leaving the seven for the eight without understanding why. Whenever you come in contact with a five, they just don't do anything for you. "Well, he is attractive and seems nice, but there is no spark." It just seems that the stripes don't match.

Excluding many of those widowed, if you are reading this and are "of a certain age" and single, you are probably not in that group of people whose imprint led them to choose the perfect mate and live happily ever after. And you are also probably denying the premise that your choices are not under your complete conscious control. That's okay. I used to think the same thing.

As I said, these choices are unavoidable and uncontrollable because they are subconscious. Well, they are until you make them conscious. I used to make those subconscious choices and wonder why I repeatedly found myself in the same circumstances. It took several years of repeating the same behaviors until I realized I was "locked" into a type. Years later, I wish I could say that conscious recognition of a subconscious influence fixes things, but it does not. Happily, though, I don't make the same mistakes as often as I used to. (I tend to hide more)

But the subconscious does like to drive - with the windows down, the radio loud, and gas to the floor.

If you have ever looked at a couple and wondered, "How on earth did THEY get together?" Now you know - Zebra Stripes.

If you have ever looked at yourself in the mirror and wondered, "How did I get myself into this?" Now you know - Zebra Stripes.

SENSUS COMMUNIS

When something positive is said about someone, you often hear, "He's got horse sense." You rarely hear, "He's got common sense." You typically hear the term "common sense" when someone says someone else "hasn't got the common sense of a billy goat." Granted, that is usually said when another person acts more like a billy goat than a human. But I think that "common sense" is a bit misunderstood.

Common sense comes from the Latin term Sensus Communis, or "community of senses." Literally, it means the "community" or collection of all that someone has sensed through taste, touch, hearing, seeing, and smelling. So, in reality, everyone has common sense. Their own, perhaps weird, form of it, at a level that may remind you more of a billy goat, but they definitely have it. Still, I haven't met any human that gives milk, has a white beard, eats tin cans, and head-butts anything that bends over in front of it. Well, Great Aunt Hilda, maybe. No, she didn't eat tin cans.

From birth, and beginning with whatever Zebra Stripes style imprinting you are exposed to, your brain senses and stores everything. Your common sense is like a database inside your brain that keeps track of everything you have sensed and thought. That way, when something comes up, your brain can access all your experiences on that subject. Like, when somebody says, "Hey, pick that up," you look around for Aunt Hilda before you bend over to get it.

Common sense is our little friend inside our head that reminds us:

Not to touch the hot stove, don't cross against traffic, say thank you, pull over when you hear a siren, don't sass your daddy, send flowers, don't put a knife in the socket, be nice to the waitress while you are still waiting for your food to come, lock your doors, and "The dog ate it" didn't work in Mrs. Johnson's English class so it definitely won't work for your wife's birthday card.

What about kids? Obviously, they don't have the breadth and depth of experience that an adult has accumulated. For every ounce of inexperience, they have a pound of curiosity. An unnamed five-year-old in my family just had to stick his finger in the light socket, knowing he had been told not to. But I didn't do it again.

Something else that really perplexed me as a child - smoking. One day, also when I was about five, I took one of my mother's cigarettes to the basement. I lit it, took one drag - just like Mom and Dad - and thought I was going to die. What were they doing to themselves when they smoked? I wouldn't stick my finger back in the light socket, and I wouldn't smoke again. The next night at the dinner table, my dad asked me if I wanted a smoke (parents know everything). I politely declined, and it was never mentioned again. But, after trying a cigarette, I just knew my parents were putting their finger in the light socket after we went to bed.

With time, kids gain experience and develop their own Common Sense databases. They learn things like:

You must be very careful with Neapolitan ice cream, or you get strawberry in with your chocolate and vanilla.

Don't let your dad talk you into tasting his green peppers - again.

Smile and act innocent after you hit your brother.

Aunt Hilda won't kiss you if you have a snake in your hands.

As they mature into teenagers, their experiences have built to the point where they can, kinda sorta, act more adult-like. For instance:

> Making their car look like it hasn't been where it has been.
>
> Making their clothes look like they haven't been where they have been.
>
> Making their little brother look like he hasn't been there with them and knowing how to bribe him into keeping quiet.

These are all skills and life lessons that many adults cling to, often to the dismay of their loved ones and colleagues.

***

I had a retail job selling tires in the 70s when checks were the primary payment method. During checkout, I had to write the customer's license number and date of birth on the back of their check. After a couple of years, I got very good at guessing the age of people because I constantly - and silently - guessed at the age before I got a license. Then, seeing the DOB gave me instant feedback. I could adjust my technique to where, over time, I was usually within two years of their age, whether they were male or female, young or old.

Another thing I learned from that job was to be careful judging by appearance. Two customers came in within a week or two of each other, which I remember because of the contrast between the two experiences. One guy was wearing a high-end designer suit and driving a newer car. The other had a ten-year-old pickup truck, and he was wearing overalls. When paying, the guy in overalls reached into the bib pocket and pulled out a wad of cash that would choke a horse. I had to cut up the credit card of the fancy suit guy.

For me, both those experiences have been equally valuable over the following years. However, the human nature side of the latter instance is more beneficial to most. Unless you work at a carnival and need to guess ages.

Speaking of ages, they can significantly affect how much data a person has saved to their common sense database. However, this is only sometimes true. Take driving, for example. A person that is forty-five years old would have far more driving experience than a twenty-eight-year-old. Right? But, let's say these two people leave home at eight AM and return home at six PM. The forty-five-year-old, Person A, has always worked his office job 10 miles from his house and spends about 30 minutes daily in his car. The twenty-eight-year-old, Person B, is in the courier business and drives eight hours a day all over town. Also, let's assume they both started this routine at age twenty. That means Person A has 3,250 hours behind the wheel for work-week driving, and Person B has 16,640.

In this case, the younger person has far more driving experience than the older and can - probably - react appropriately to more circumstances due to a more significant amount of driving data stored away. Person A - probably - has broader life experiences than Person B and is likely to respond better than Person B in many other situations. So, age is a significant factor in many day-to-day facets of life but not always an indicator of the value of what gets stored in the database for a particular subject.

Some data may not come from personal experience of doing, but from things a person has witnessed or been told about. Of course, second-hand and third-hand experiences still go into the database since they are obtained via your senses. Since we are humans, we can imagine. We can take a first-hand, observed, or related experience and think about what we might do when faced with the same circumstance. That thought exercise will then become more information in your database.

Whether driving, cooking, working, or whatever it may be, all you sense becomes part of your common sense database. In this way, you are absolutely unique. On the other hand, most people with similar geography or culture have a significant number of experiences in common. And the "commonality" of most people's "common sense" makes life and society work, all while allowing for individual differences. Common sense would tell you that the grocery store is busiest on Saturday afternoons. For some, that is a reason to avoid the store. Another person may have met their loving spouse in a crowded store on Saturday. For them, the hustle and bustle may provide a very positive feeling.

Amongst the mass of information that your senses take in, and despite the commonality mentioned above, there are outlier events which are more unique items that a comparatively small number of people experience. Depending on the nature of the experience, these outlier events can have an outsized influence on how a person processes their common sense database.

For instance, a person who has been the victim of a sexual assault may be unable to stand in the kitchen with their back to the window unless the curtain is drawn. A person that has been in combat may become nervous or upset at loud or violent movies. In these and many other circumstances, good and bad, the unique experience can become a factor in every seemingly unrelated decision.

A reasonably well-adjusted person typically knows when they are around someone that appears similar in intelligence and social understanding. When you meet someone of this ilk, you may have initial expectations that they will have an amount of like-mindedness with you. But you notice that whenever you say, metaphorically speaking, that something is "round," they then say it is "oval." Black is white, and so on. The person may have a unique experience that they are factoring into the mix that you cannot understand.

When something like this happens, it is easy to insist that you are right and they are wrong. If you are paying attention to life, you have probably noticed that telling people they are wrong gets you nowhere, fast. It is better to be aware this type of disconnect can occur when interacting with others so you can recognize it and disengage. When disengaging is not an option, change the tactics used when dealing with the person. The main thing is to understand that, as similar as our common sense databases are to each other, the profoundly personal and unique stuff can get in the way.

◆ ◆ ◆

People in their twenties are definitely adults, but my common sense tells me that you are somewhere around thirty before you have, shall we say, "settled" into adulthood, with plenty of adult experiences and responsibilities neatly tucked under your belt. Unless something interrupts your usual way of thinking, such as a brain injury or dementia, you will continue adding to the database your entire life.

Most of your continued experiences will be "more of the same" and affirming of that settled person you are. A new job, a new vacation spot, or a new sweetheart may work to change your outlook. Still, it will not likely change anything significant about your worldview.

Through the everyday accumulation of experiences or, perhaps, some more momentous occurrence, you may change your mind about something that you thought was a relatively settled matter. A firmly held belief or even a vital component of your "self" becomes outdated. This is because your common sense has added enough data to the contrary of that belief to change the result of your internal calculation

Even a significant change in our "self" will soon become just more of the same in our huge mental database. And with all that data stored away, we can draw upon dozens, maybe hundreds, of memories about particular and related subjects to get us through each step of our daily lives, hopefully without touching a hot stove.

As common things go, common sense is a standout.

SIXTH SENSE

As we mature into adults, we have hopefully developed a reasonable Common Sense database. We move through life equipped to respond to most of life's trials, temptations, and victories without any research, such as reading an etiquette handbook before deciding to use a fork or spoon on peas. If you must, keep the smartphone out of sight of the other guests.

Assuming you are not a billy goat, your common sense will be the old-fashioned human being kind, obtained through your senses and stored away for future use. People can have widely diverse experiences that can affect the amount and quality of the data in the common sense database. This can account for the differences in the ability to draw reasonable conclusions faced with the same or similar circumstances. It might take one person two or three experiences of an event to reach a sound judgment, and another person five and another ten. That may be why so many people have been married so many times.

Your brain, being the powerhouse it is, can store phenomenal amounts of information and then, upon stimulus, sort and collate that information to then be processed by your reasoning faculties. The beautiful part about this database is that it not only keeps words, numbers, and pictures - it keeps them in full-motion 3-D video complete with voice inflection, emotion, attendant circumstances, and your own response or feelings about the remembered event.

For instance, you look up at the sky, your mind sorts through the "pictures" it has for the sky and finds matches for the conditions you see. You then reason that when you have seen the sky like this in the past, certain weather conditions are present. And you will probably be as accurate as the National Weather Service. Based on the cumulative experiences from his past projects, a carpenter can look at the grain of a piece of wood and know if it will work for his new project. A gardener can look at a plant and tell if it is getting too much sunlight. Your mom can thump a cantaloupe and tell how ripe it is. A doctor can look at an X-ray and - "Hey, this liver looks like the 9th hole at Augusta."

Well, enough of that. I am sure you get the picture. If you get the picture, it is because the stimulus I have provided has worked on your common sense database to use your experiences to access related memories.

Speaking of pictures. And please bear with this analogy. It seems technical at first glance, but it is an excellent illustration of the point, and I promise it will be over quickly!

The resolution of computer monitors and TVs has evolved and significantly improved since the 1980s. Most monitors started with 640x480 resolution, spent a long stretch at 1024x768, and are now at 1920x1080 (hence the 1080p you see on product descriptions). These dimensions represent the number of pixels in width and height. The total number of pixels on the screen is obtained by multiplying the two numbers. So a 640x480 screen has about 307,000 pixels, 1024x768 has about 785,000, and 1920x1080 has over 2,000,000 pixels. This means the 1920x1080 screen has nearly 7 times the pixels, and therefore detail, than 640x480. Not to mention 4k resolution. Oy ve!

And, in today's mature television and computer age, most people know or have heard of RGB video signals. RGB stands for Red/Green/Blue, the main colors from which all other colors on the screen are derived. As just discussed, a digital LED television or computer monitor screen has hundreds of thousands or millions of pixels, and each pixel has a red, green, and blue component. The intensity of each of the three colors determines the pixel's viewable color. Then, all the thousands of pixels combine to create the whole image you watch on the TV.

Now. Think of your brain as the monitor screen and the common sense database experiences as if they were all pixels, with each additional data point adding to the resolution or available information. And depending on the person's intellect, the intensity and brightness of the "colors" lend to the quality of the image. So, you not only have the quantity of "pixels" in the picture but also the "quality" of the individual pixel.

Once it has received a stimulus, the brain will recall, sort, and process all its associated data on the subject of the trigger event and then build a picture in response. This is where "common sense" is more Sensus Communis, which is more about the individual than the commonality between individuals.

Looking first at quantity, one person's experience regarding a subject may be less than the next person's. This can result in a pixel "resolution" more like the 640x480 monitor we discussed above, as opposed to the other person's resolution of 1024x768. Then another person, perhaps the courier driver we discussed, will have substantially greater experience to draw from. For driving, we could say that he has a resolution of 1920x1080.

For quality, we all know from life that "some people never learn," and regardless of how often they do something, they make the same mistakes repeatedly. This is where the quality of intellect comes into play. The "brightness" of the event, the recognition of its significance, may not be as strong as for someone else. This makes their "picture" less sharp and less valuable for decision-making. Whereas another person of higher intellect may experience the image in the full effect of its quantity and quality.

So, at one end of the spectrum, you can end up with someone with low resolution and low brightness. On the other end, high resolution and brightness. That low-resolution/low-brightness person is probably the one that gets mentioned with billy goats.

You have likely seen movies where the police or some spy agency put someone's picture on the left side of a monitor screen. The right side of the monitor has a series of images of known criminals flashing by until the software finds a "match" for the picture on the left. Think of the brain comparing data, just like in the movie. The currently sensed image is on the left side of the brain's projection screen. All the related information from the common sense database is compared and processed on the right side of the screen.

Once the matching and relevant bits of information are sorted, the brain reviews all the attendant information attached to those previous experiences. It then starts feeding your conscious level with conclusions or assumptions based on those experiences. Sometimes you get a perfect match, like seeing someone with a gun and the gun fires. You know the resulting sound is from the weapon. Your brain will likely feed you a conclusion/assumption that immediate danger exists. The following conclusion/assumption is usually to go change your underwear.

Sometimes you hear a loud noise but don't see where it comes from. Depending on the noise, your brain may conclude some level of danger and tell you to be startled. It may not. Depending on how often you have heard a gun fire, a tire blow out, or an exploding power transformer, your brain may or may not automatically recognize the sound as a particular event or, when it does, cause you to respond defensively.

These are clearly obvious examples. Not so obvious, and sometimes seemingly mystical, are times when you observe someone and, for some reason, you know what they do for a living or maybe what part of the country they are from. This is not because you are psychic. It is because the person has done or said something, which you may not be consciously aware of, that reminds you of similar attributes you have previously observed. Observations that you were able to connect with a particular profession, etc.

There are constantly circumstances where you may only have, for example, three out of five of the pieces of data necessary for a "perfect match." But, each time, your brain will assess the currently available information and provide you with the most likely assumption(s) based on your experience database. And, quite often, your "most likely assumptions" are correct. Your ability to make observations of this type is greatly affected by how well the senses "focus" all their current and past data on the screen for comparison.

Depending on the extent of your experiences and clarity of mind, you may make observational assumptions that lesser experienced people think to be "psychic." But we know better. You have likely seen some TV show or movie where the con man can pick up on essential details about someone just from a momentary glance, then use those details to their advantage.

The con man or the "brilliant detective" character is excellent at what they do. The capabilities portrayed on the screen are overstated, but a person can be nearly as skilled in real life. This skill is not from a mere "willingness" to see detail but from long-term practice and, usually, a need. Real con men, fortune tellers, and the like use their talents to allow them a chance to have the knowledge to control the other players in their scenario.

The ability of some to properly use their data may be affected by many factors. The isolation from lack of exposure to others as someone grows up can limit the experiences or resolution of someone's database. A physiological degradation in mental capacity has a significant effect, of course. In immediate terms, this focus is affected by alcohol or drugs, lack of sleep, preoccupation with other matters, or merely a lack of interest. Your willingness to exercise your abilities makes a considerable difference in the outcome.

The "sixth sense" claimed by many is often called ESP or "extrasensory perception," implying that one can gain input through means other than the five senses. From my point of view, the sixth sense is merely the juncture at which all the five senses come together with the common sense database to form a conclusion beyond the immediately obvious, allowing the "whole" to become greater than the sum of the parts. Rather than extrasensory perception, it may more aptly be referred to as extraordinary perception.

THE FORMULA

We have discussed 1) the imprinting that occurs from birth, 2) the fact that the brain stores and uses all your experiences as the Sensus Communis, 3) the capability of your mind to respond to a stimulus and gather all the related experiences to form a mental picture of what your brain thinks of that stimulus and 4) what, if any, reaction is most appropriate.

What do we call it when people use their experiences about a particular subject to make better decisions? That sounds like wisdom to me.

More often than not, when the word "wisdom" is used, it refers to a person using wisdom to guide them through something difficult. We may not all be Solomon, but most of us can, eventually, take a breath and allow our mind a chance to save us from ourselves.

On the other hand...

- You may have an expectation of being able to play the piano. If you have no training or experience, you will likely be disappointed when you perform for your friends.
- You may set out to build a piece of furniture, expecting it to be beautiful and functional. Regardless of the expensive tools you have filled your basement with, if you have no training or experience in woodworking, you are likely to be disappointed with the outcome.
- You see a pickup truck with a sign on the side that says "PLUMBER," and ask the driver to replace your water heater and repair a few leaks. What could go wrong?

- You are sitting at dinner with someone you just met, and they have a great car, a great smile, and a great job. You start thinking about the future. What could go wrong?

Oh? You don't want to drop relationships in the middle of all those other examples? It does kind of kill the buzz, doesn't it?

But. Wisdom is grounded in reality. It looks at past experiences and pays little attention to what you wanted... only to what you got. Wisdom trods heavily on the eggshells of life that your expectations walk so lightly upon.

So, you are still at dinner with your first date. You both love moonlight and long walks on the beach. "Where has this person been all my life? I can't wait to wake up early on Saturday morning and have coffee on the patio with this person. The future is so bright!"

If I could have sound effects, this is where that sound of a needle scratching across a record would come in. You know. They use that sound all the time on TV shows.

You had it. All you had to do was stop at "Where has this person been all my life?" That is the question that needs to be answered, and it will take a long time to find the answer to that one question. There are hundreds of things to know about someone before you say, "The future looks bright."

What happened?

It is just me here, so I will answer. You allowed yourself to have expectations you had no business having. You have no more business thinking about the future with a person while on a first date than you have a chance of playing Beethoven's Fifth when you have yet to have piano lessons.

And that is the rub, is it not? Those pesky expectations.

Through many errors in judgment and observations of the same, I have devised a formula that helps a person manage expectations. This is applicable whether your expectations are romantic in nature or related to hiring a plumber, for that matter. It applies to any relationship you can have.

$$\text{Probability of Disappointment} = \frac{\text{Expectations}}{\text{Experience}}$$

Mathematically, this says that the Probability of Disappointment is equal to Expectations divided by Experience. I wonder if they still teach this, but when I was in school, we could also say it: Expectations over Experience. I like that because it is correct mathematically and alludes to how some may order the importance. Division still applies, but we must figure out some numbers to use first.

Before that, I am assuming you don't like to be disappointed. Am I correct? I know we are all disappointed occasionally, especially when things happen that are out of our control. And sometimes things go wrong in situations over which we do have control. When that happens, we are disappointed by the outcome <u>and</u> the fact that we were part of the problem. But we are reasonable people, so we know there is some risk of disappointment in any situation where we are looking for a positive outcome.

In my formula, the optimal number for the Probability of Disappointment (PoD) is 1, which requires that Expectations and Experience be the same value. Scales from one to ten are easy to work with, so to get a PoD of 1, your Expectations/Experience numbers could be 1/1. 2/2, 5/5, and so forth. The idea here is that to have a reasonable PoD, your expectations of a given person or situation should be gauged by your experience with that person or situation. If you have zero experience with someone, then you should have zero expectations of them or close to zero.

Let's go back to the first date scenario. If you have been sitting with someone for an hour and are already thinking, "The future is bright," then I think we can give the Expectations a value of 7. If this is the first date and you haven't spent time with them,

I will be generous and assign your Experience level a 1. This is based on whatever got you to the point of spending an hour with your date.

In this scenario, then your PoD is 7. You may have had a few extended phone calls before this date. Ok, give it an Experience of 2. Then the PoD is 3.5. Still a high Probability of Disappointment for someone new. If you never hear from this person again after the end of the date, you will likely spend some time and/or emotion thinking about the matter. It may even affect you for a few days.

But let's say you are sitting there and enjoying the company of someone new, and you came in with appropriate expectations. You are both inquisitive of the other and find each other engaging. With each question or story shared, you increase your experience with this person. But, for our numbering system, we are talking decimal points, not whole digits. After three questions in a row, your Experience and Expectations increase ever so slightly. That fourth question, though, they blew it. Experience goes up, and Expectations may drop back a little. But, as long as that last one wasn't a "deal breaker," you keep talking. As the night goes on, the Experience meter will keep edging up. Hopefully, the Expectation meter will regulate itself as the adrenaline of excitement wears off.

If you are on a date, you are probably at least somewhat hopeful for the future and would like to see your expectations piqued. As I mentioned, I think the optimal PoD is 1, but what if someone comes in with lower expectations than usual? As in, "Dates always turn out bad for me." As bad as a high PoD is, if someone is on a date and has such low expectations that their PoD is less than 1, I wonder how they get out of bed in the morning.

Remember that this is the Probability of Disappointment... not Definite Disappointment. And it is a good idea to revisit the formula occasionally and ensure you, like wisdom, are grounded in reality.

I don't mean to raise your expectations, but this formula can help lower expectations... and in a good way. Think about the formula for areas of your life besides dating relationships. You can apply it to home repairs, TV shows, things you buy online, new restaurants, buying new clothes... all kinds of things. The more you take a moment to balance your expectations with your experiences, the more satisfied you will be with your decisions. Less regret in life is a good thing.

SECTION II: RELATIONSHIPS

Now that you know the biased basic basis for all things interpersonal, let's move to the specifics.

My daughter, in her own teenage* wisdom, thought of a great way to improve life in the "relationship" arena. Everyone would have a sign above their head. On the sign there would be three lights and written next to each light would be "I like you," "Let's be friends" and "Please go away." Then, when talking to someone of the opposite sex, the appropriate light would automatically come on for how the person really feels at the moment.

I don't have any new body technology to help with such things, but I have a few ideas and observations about relationships and how people interact.

*My daughter is now almost the age that I was when I wrote down what she said. Where does the time go?

CARE*

wouldn't it be nice to,

even just every now and then,

lay in someone's arms, be perfectly

still and feel safe, cared for, watched over

and the only expectation for that moment is that

the other feels the same.

I have a bird feeder on the patio outside my kitchen window. Though other birds occasionally come around, it attracts cardinals more than others. All birds are nervous creatures, but cardinals seem edgier than most. I see the cardinals alone most of the time. Sometimes the male, sometimes the female. When I see the birds eating solo, he or she will peck at the seed, look up and around, peck again, and look up and around again. They seem to spend more time looking around for danger than eating.

One day I was looking out the window and noticed the pair together. The male was sitting on the eave of the roof, just a few feet above and to the side of the feeder, constantly looking around. The female was on the feeder and would peck and then peck again. I watched her for a while, and it was at least a minute before she even looked up from the seed. Eventually, the male took off, with the female right behind him. Since then, there have been times when the male was on the feeder, and the female took the lookout position above. The male seemed equally content with the situation, not looking up nearly as often as he would have if alone.

Nature is pretty simple. Man is complicated.

WANTED: A GOOD MAN WITH A CHAINSAW*

While out for the evening, I ran into a friend who was with several of her friends. I met everyone and did my best to keep up with nine new names (alliterative, eh?), but even the great Stan sometimes falls short. I was quickly admonished for getting one of the names wrong in an e-mail. I usually do well with names, though. I have been on several cruises and typically get the nine new names at the dinner table memorized within five minutes. Then I start guessing where people are from. I usually cruise alone, so my table mates sometimes think I must be part of the ship's entertainment. I try not to guess weights, though... especially toward the end of the cruise.

That night, after the introductions were made and names were forgotten, the group dynamics adjusted, and people returned to regular conversation. I was talking with my friend and her date. I don't see this woman often, so I wasn't sure how long they had been dating or how serious they were. In times like these, it would be easier to catch up if there was a set numerical designation for the current status of a relationship. We could use something like, "Hi. This is my date, Fred. We are currently a 12 on the Relationship Intensity scale." On a 30-point scale, I think a 12 would be somewhere around the point of "I haven't met his family yet, but his teenager answered the phone the other day, and she knew who I was." Come to think of it, the one or two times my daughter answered the phone and talked to someone I had been dating, she just told them to run. I will have to remember to change the will.

As we all talked, the woman next to me told one of the others that, right now, she needed a "good man with a chainsaw." I have heard a lot of wish lists... but a chainsaw was a new one. She had a couple of trees down in her yard and needed help getting them taken care of. I thought about it and considered that we all have probably adjusted what we "think" we want in someone of the opposite sex based on what our practical needs are at the moment.

I was sprucing up my patio area and buying plants and flowers at the landscape place. I am not experienced in getting all the heights of the plants arranged and laid out where the end result looks good. Last year I planted a bed, and four weeks later, the three rows were neatly stair-cased from front to back. In four more weeks, the second row was so tall that you couldn't see the back row.

So there I was, standing in the garden department, other customers noticing the glaze over my eyes. I thought, "Right now, I could use a 'good woman' that knows flowers." Of course, it also crossed my mind that maybe a "bad" woman that knows flowers would be a plus. After all, you can't garden all the time.

Though a bit unrealistic, picking particular attributes for people as we move through various stages and times would be nice. Someone that can garden in the spring, someone that looks good in a bathing suit for the summer, someone that likes to hike in the mountains in the fall, and someone that wants to chop firewood in the winter. What a woman.

In the meantime, I personally can move fallen trees with pure mental concentration... and a phone call to the tree guys.

PROS OR CONS

People constantly get information from their senses and then continuously process and evaluate it. In the grocery store, we pick bananas based on our experience and preference for the peel's green-to-brown spectrum. We look at the marbling or grain on a steak and can assume specific characteristics of the cooked product. Asparagus, for me, is judged by the diameter of the stalk. I like the smaller ones.

We do the same thing with people on the street, with our co-workers, our friends, and especially when it comes to those we date. There are hundreds of features, physical and otherwise, that could be listed, but here are a few that come to mind. Your list is what matters.

This story is not a story with a point as much as it is a reference point, so you understand when "the list" of features is referred to elsewhere. Don't worry. There won't be a test. Think of it as auditing a 101 class.

Height	Intelligence
Weight	Handy with Tools
Age	Politeness
Income	Kind of Car
Physique	Kind of House
Strength	Clothing
Hair Color	Kissing
Hair Absence	Sex Compatibility
Kind Eyes	Sex Drive
Wit	Manners

Religion	Sense of Humor
Cooking	Compassion
Neatness	Consideration of Others
Grooming	Drugs
Alcohol	Red or White Wine
Vocabulary	Talkative
Occupation	Respectful
Simple or Fine Dining	Types of Movies
Well Read	Sensitivity

As you read this list, you are undoubtedly thinking of your list and how it may differ from these items. Likely, you are also thinking of the importance you give each of these features when you meet someone that interests you. You probably already know which of these are essential triggers for you, good or bad. If you don't, you should definitely keep reading these stories.

Another point. Anything in the list that is relevant is also relative. Usually. My idea of "talkative" may differ from yours. "Someone tall" may mean someone 5'10". For the next person, it may be at least 6'2". Once again - your list. Only you can judge. Familiarity with this concept is handy when a friend is setting you up. Your friend's idea of a "good cook" may be based on the lack of subsequent hospital visits.

Just keep "the list" in mind, as it does come up here and there. I said there wouldn't be a test, but there is an exam each time you mentally evaluate another person. And you are not just putting the other person to the test, but also your awareness of your needs. The good part is you can retake the test as often as you care to.

DANCING AS ONE

As often happens, one night, I was at one of my favorite piano bars, listening to my friend Bob entertain. An older gentleman, somewhere in his seventies, came up to the piano and was swaying to the music. He seemed to enjoy himself, and as soon as Bob finished the tune he was playing, the man asked for a song that seemed odd for a fellow his age to ask for, but musical tastes know no boundaries.

The man moved back down with his family members and began to dance when Bob started to play the song. At first, he danced with a woman I guessed was his daughter. Of course, I assumed that from her age. I could have easily been wrong since, when it comes to the age difference in a relationship, again, there are no boundaries. A moment or two later, a woman I assumed was his wife walked up, and they started dancing. There was no more guessing... It was apparent as soon as they locked into each other for the dance. As they danced, they danced as one. It was quite apparent they had been doing this together for a long time.

As soon as I saw them fall into the natural rhythm of their dancing together, I remembered another time I saw this so vividly in an older couple. It was in January of 1994. I was on a cruise... my first. My divorce had been final in September of the previous year. Between work and "domestic realignments," I was absolutely worn out. I wondered what I could do by myself that would be relaxing yet not dull or isolated. Someone suggested a cruise, and I was on the boat two weeks later.

One of the nights, there was a Captain's Reception in the showroom, and I went just to have the experience... and the free drinks. After the hors d'oeuvres and champagne, the captain spoke a little and announced that the orchestra would play for a while and the stage would be open for dancing. I stuck around for a few minutes to listen to the music and to see what would happen. The orchestra started playing a tune from the 40s. One of those "Big Band" tunes you can never remember the name of... but is on every one of those Big Band compilation CDs advertised on late-night TV. I would hum it for you, but I haven't figured out how to do that in writing yet.

As twenty or thirty couples made their way to the dance floor, I noticed one in particular. They appeared to easily be in their seventies, and he had to have been at least six inches shorter than she. I thought, "How odd?" and then they started dancing. It was as if they melted together, right there on the stage... and they started moving as one person. I don't remember ever seeing, or at least noticing, something like that before. They gazed into each other's eyes, which should have been a strain with the height difference. But it wasn't. Then they would spin around and move across the floor in a way that had everything you always saw in the movies, plus one more thing. They were in love.

As I said before, I had only been divorced a couple of months and didn't have a steady footing in my life then. But I saw something in the couple on the floor that I knew I wanted in my life. I didn't know when, but I knew that I would not settle for anything less than to someday be able to dance with someone like that... as one person.

And here I was, nine years later, watching a repeat of that night on the ship. I certainly didn't know the couple. I didn't know how long they had been together. I didn't know what kind of life they had together. But one thing was crystal clear. They danced together. They loved dancing together. They moved as one person.

BALANCE

In many movies or TV shows about the "old days," there is quite often a couple of days of mud, murder, and mayhem capped off with a gunfight that decides the fate of the West. And quite often, the leading man is a cowboy who meets the town doctor's sister or some similarly available woman. Amid all the shoot-em-up, the cowboy almost always decides he has fallen in love with the woman after barely spending time in the same room. The first issue of their new love soon arises in some comic scene in which they argue about who will tell whom to do what.

In almost all the old and some new movies, characters meet, fall in love, and decide to get married, all within a period that can be measured in hours rather than months or years. I guess that was how it was back when things were "simpler"... when people only needed to recognize that they were attracted to each other and assumed a lifelong commitment would be no trouble. And, in an age when both men and women "knew their places," it probably was easier to accept a mate based on purely initial attraction, especially since a lifelong commitment, after all, was a lifelong commitment.

In this scenario, the cowboy always wins because the man is "in charge." In a relationship not built on anything but attraction and a promise, there must be a leader and a follower, as only an utterly one-sided relationship could ever work in such a circumstance. This marriage would have no "honey, what do you think?"

Over a few hundred years, things have changed a bit, and couples often attempt to find a balance in their interactions. It wasn't that 200 years ago a woman didn't want more say. It was that societal norms would not allow. Of course, those societal norms were structured by men. In today's society, women are more broadly assertive, but some women and some men still think along the old ways.

I have seen plenty of examples of men and women who still think and act the same way as the characters in the movie example. And that is primarily that the man does not care what the woman thinks, and the woman doesn't care what the man wants. They are both still acting in a primal fashion, with the man geared toward sex and possession and the woman geared toward comfort and safety. Of course, people like this are not looking for balance.

Life is easy if you're looking for a needle in the haystack but will settle for a straw. Many people take that path of least resistance. At some point, though, you begin looking for balance and want to avoid spending time in imbalanced situations. For that, it is essential to know not only what we want in another but, very specifically, what we don't want, the deal breakers.

After over 20 years of dating, my deal breakers and preferences have become tightly defined. That is not to say I don't step outside the box occasionally. But, each time I do, I have renewed respect for my prior decisions. I am still a man, and the old ways are hard to shake. But, more and more, I think about what tomorrow morning may bring as opposed to merely what tonight may offer. Though this has severely cut into my sex life, it is easier to wake up and deal with a hangover than a stay-over.

In a new relationship, getting to know someone and seeing their true nature takes a long time. Confounding the flow of "getting to know you" is that most people are not consciously aware of their deepest feelings about relationships and how men and women should interact. Even worse, one may only realize the nature of those deep-rooted feelings once married. We act more consciously and in the moment as we date and become more and more involved. But, as soon as the marriage switch is flipped, we revert to the only true example we have in our deepest psyche - the standard of our parents. That can be a good thing or a bad thing. This may explain why so many couples that have lived together for a while end up divorced shortly after marriage. Expectations change and, soon after, the dynamics of the relationship.

I will get back to the point. I was speaking about balance and how some people do not use balance as the basis for choosing another. Yes, friends often chide me for my strict list of deal breakers and preferences. On the other end of the spectrum, I have known people who would go out with almost anybody who asks, with no qualification process, and then wonder why they keep repeating the same mistakes. It is easier to disregard balance since, to find balance, you must bring out the scales. But not bathroom scales, where you are only weighing yourself. I mean balance scales, where you consider or evaluate one side compared to the other.

Like most single people in this technological age, I have visited online dating sites. Some profiles I read are precise in what the person is looking for and their desires in a relationship. Others are jokingly lacking. I have often been struck by the apparent laziness of the person that needs to work on their woefully incomplete profile. Do they actually not care about their intended's height, weight, religion, or intellectual prowess, as long as they like puppies?

In a previous chapter, Pros or Cons, I list some of the typical "features" we recognize in others. When using the scales as a mental or written exercise, you add or remove from each side of the scale based on the value the "feature" has for you. For instance, one person may find another person's vanity a negative feature. Someone else may find vanity a plus. The same could be said for education or income. Note - This is where you would give whatever weight you deem appropriate to "liking puppies."

In the movie, our leading man and woman would never check the scales for balance. Since both parties subconsciously knew the relationship would be based on power and manipulation, why bother? With no intention of either party expecting or offering balance, no measuring device is necessary.

Parity is a word I like to use when determining balance in a relationship. It carries the idea that two people may not bring the same things to the table... but an equivalency. You bring a pound. I bring 16 ounces. Neither party has a dominance that can be wielded in times of trouble. Communication and compromise become all important.

I am enough of a romantic to believe that though love does not conquer all, it can be used on the scales. You can achieve parity without achieving perfect balance. And, once you achieve parity, you don't have to balance every time; we balance over time.

Where should balance and parity start? In the beginning. A tightrope walker doesn't wait until they are halfway across the Grand Canyon to get their balance. They start off balanced and remain balanced, or they fail. It is difficult to pay attention to balance and deal-breakers when you are in the throes of some physical or "zebra-stripe" induced attraction. But this is where balance is the most important, as it sets the tone for everything that comes after.

A couple, ok three, things to remember.

1) Don't bother with this if you are just looking for a good time and a couple of passionate weekends. Your main objective with that is to ensure you don't end up in a compost pile in the woods.

2) However, if you are even slightly entertaining something longer term, pay attention to balance. If you bring out the scales and heed the results, you will end some relationships.

3) In longer-term relationships, occasionally bring out the scales, recheck for balance, and be aware of any changes in your feelings of parity.

DAN BAILEY

And no thumbs on the scales!

YIN AND YANG

Most are familiar with the Taijitu symbol, which represents the concept of Yin and Yang. Yin and Yang can be applied to many pairs in life, such as night and day or opposite yet interdependent. But outside of Chinese philosophy, we most often see it used in relation to male and female duality. Reducing the concept's meaning to the male/female duality inevitably leads to references about conflict with themes of butting heads and the like with the opposite sex.

When we start talking about the opposite sex, social conditioning usually makes us focus on the "opposing sex" rather than the opposite. This makes for great rom-com movie plots as the grain of truth is there. The symbol, though, illustrates the idea of the opposite yet equal. Not fighting. But nesting.

Setting aside the "opposite" factor for a moment, note how the sides are identical in shape and fully merge to create the whole circle. Of course, this represents the male and female concept as a whole. We all know that on an individual basis, there are significant differences from person to person, and there are plenty of Yangs out there that your Yin wouldn't even think about fully merging with. But, when two people get into a long-term relationship, get married, or date for months or years, the idea of equal but opposite comes into play in a significant way.

We have all seen couples that we thought just didn't fit. Whether a perceived disparity in attractiveness or, if we know one or both, a mismatch in personality. We see them together and say, "I just don't get it." But people tend to find their own balance one way or another. Whenever you think that Yin you saw at the store has something you don't believe Yang has a match for, there is something about Yang that Yin values in a way you don't see. And sometimes, you don't want to know what it is. That boils down to perspective, which I discuss in another section. You cannot understand what is going on when you don't see things from the same place as those you are trying to figure out.

DATING

In my mind's eye of people who have been single for a while, I visualize a line of people, with each reaching out to the person in front of them, not one of them realizing that if they would just turn around, someone would be there for them.

Most of this book is about relationships in one way or another, but here are a few thoughts particular to dating.

What Is It Gonna Take?

I can't tell you how many times I have heard people, even so-called dating gurus, say, "When dating, you really need to know what you want in a person." And I agree it is a good idea to know what you want.

For discussion, let's say there are ten main things about people, features if you will, that we pay attention to when dating. Height, Weight, Car, Job, Income, Sense of Humor, etc. You know what you want. You want a guy over six feet that makes a good living and dresses nicely. Not too hard; you can see two out of three when you first lay eyes on him, and he is driving a brand new sports car, indicating he must make a good living. Not bad. Bring on the martinis. (Guys do the same thing, of course.)

And you go on four or five more dates and find out he has been divorced for two months and has two kids in elementary school. Your two kids are in their late 20s. You quit seeing him. But... didn't he have the features you were looking for?

Some people date just so they won't be alone or because they want to have sex. Granted... Both are noble causes. Or maybe you go by the old saying, "You have to kiss a few frogs." But, really, do you like kissing frogs? What if you, as your dating profile says, are looking for a long-term relationship?

After kissing my share of frogs, not that there is anything wrong with that, I decided that knowing what I want is not the most important thing when it comes to dating. In my experience, it is more important to understand what you don't want. Do you know what your "deal-breakers" are?

I think you do... if you have dated for a while. Little kids in school. No thanks. Adult kids living at home. Ditto. Drugs. Not gonna happen. Divorced two months. Nah. Incompatible in politics and/or religion. Please let the night end. I see you thinking. You do know your deal-breakers.

So, you know what you don't want. Don't meet for drinks; meet for coffee. And after you have cut through the social niceties, be bold and get to the point. Ask about your deal breakers and invite them to ask you about theirs. If they have any of your deal breakers, politely leave. You don't have to impugn their dignity, just say that you don't think you are suited for each other, but leave. Save yourself and them time and emotion.

Let's face it. The person you are sitting with has already passed a few of your internal tests, or you wouldn't be there to begin with. And the longer you stay, the more you talk about what you like than what you dislike. Once you have locked onto the companionship of the moment, that deal-breaker just keeps fading away.

My motto is, "I will do whatever it takes to not get what I don't want." Like anyone, I have slipped occasionally, but this "rule" has kept me out of a lot of difficulty.

The thing that happens with many people - me included - is that in the beginning, we focus on the one or two things that we find extremely attractive about a person when we should be looking at about, my favorite example, ten things. We tend to project our positive feelings about those essential things onto the other eight things we ignore. Like, 1) she may have a great body, and 2) she may be intelligent and conversant. So, we are visually stimulated and intellectually stimulated. We like that so much that we ignore the fact that she talks badly about other people and tends to be impolite to the waiter.

You could think of many similar combinations that suit your experience. The bottom line is that, eventually, being polite to those we interact with is essential. Being negative about other people is not what you want to hear when you are together. But we ignore those things because we want to focus on the attributes that bring us the most positive feelings - at the moment. We do this even when we internally recognize that "this person" offends our sensibilities regularly.

Contractual Beings

Hammurabi, the king of ancient Babylon, had a stone pillar erected in their equivalent of the town square. On this pillar, a group of laws and punishments were engraved so that all could know what was expected of them and what they could expect if the Code of Hammurabi was violated.

Some ladies will disagree but hear me out on this point.

Setting aside the liars and cheats, I maintain that men are generally contractual beings. By that, I mean that men's intentions are 1) to do what they say they will do and 2) to not be expected to do something they have not agreed to.

The first is simple enough... They either do or they don't. The second is more complicated, at least for some women I have talked to over the years. I understand that once people start dating, there will be certain expectations. But unlike in Babylon, nothing is set in stone.

Your expectations may be reasonable. There are things that are done in polite society, after all. However, we cannot read each other's minds, and, in this case, great expectations can lead to great disappointment, as we discussed in the Irwinian Theorem > The Formula. The only rules that govern a relationship are the ones you agree to.

A female friend was telling me about having this type of misunderstanding with the guy she was dating. She had told him what she expected about something, but he didn't do what she wanted. I asked her if he actively agreed to what she had asked. She perked up a bit and said that he had not and likely side-stepped the issue in his mind. I told her I thought that he should have said something if he disagreed, but he was probably trying to avoid the conflict of saying no.

The point here, and this applies to both sexes, is that we should be aware that our romantic partners may think that something is not an issue, and that consideration should be made when one feels slighted in this way.

Taking Care Of The Self

If you are actively pursuing dating, then it probably seems that you spend a good deal of time finding someone to date, and when you do, you then spend your time working on the relationship. But what about you?

Somewhere in all the ups, downs, and sideways of trying to turn strangers into significant others, you have to take care of yourself. Stay home alone one night, walk, or go out with other friends. You have to treat yourself well, or you may be unable to sustain the pace. And this may turn into frustration with the relationship. It would be a waste to end a relationship when a little self-governance may be the key.

Also, don't be afraid to be alone. If you can be happy and secure alone, that is when you are at your best for making good choices about the person you want to spend time with. If you value yourself - all by yourself - then you only spend time with people that add to your life.

I delve deeper into these ideas in Thoughts > Self-Centered or Selfish.

Takeaways

Honesty is not the presence of perfection but the absence of deception.

Insist on treating yourself well, and others will follow your example.

Do whatever it takes to not get what you don't want.

JUST A LITTLE NERVOUS

One night I was sitting at a neighborhood restaurant bar that I frequent. A friend was sitting on my right side, and a lady I didn't know was sitting to my left. After I said hello to my friend, I turned to the lady and said hello to her. She immediately started being chatty and soon said she was "a little nervous" since she was waiting to meet a blind date. My friend and I talked with her about how she had come to meet this person. She said she had spoken to him on the phone a few times, but this was the first time they were to meet face-to-face.

While we all talked, she said again how she was nervous about the meeting and hoped it didn't show too much. I suggested that when her date arrived, she might want to say, "Hey, I am a little nervous." She looked at me with a perplexed look that matched my friend's, both seeming to question the wisdom of such a statement. I told her she could remove most of the worry of "being found out" by admitting her nervousness. Lay it out there.

People often become nervous from the excitement and apprehension of face-to-face meetings, whether a new date, a sales presentation, asking for a raise, or speaking before a group. The initial nervousness or stress can be positive because it heightens your senses in a way that allows you to take in more information and process it more quickly.

I told them that, in general, the thing that makes most people nervous is whether the other person will be able to know that they are worried. That nervousness or fear then makes you more anxious. Then, you are even more fearful of the other person noting your apprehension. (It is about this time that most of us order a second drink).

So. When you look at someone and say, "You know. I am a little nervous."... what happens? Though it will vary from person to person, you may eliminate most of the nervousness you have created for yourself, allowing you to relax back to a more normal level. The odds are heavily in your favor that if you are nervous, the other person is also likely to be. By admitting your nervousness, the other person may relax, knowing they are not alone and, hopefully, will confess their apprehensions to you. You can imagine how much more relaxed a conversation can be with most of the stress of the situation either removed or even turned into a topic that allows you both to laugh.

There is a significant secondary benefit of this self-confession. When you admit your nervousness, you are, in a sense, admitting a mild fault about yourself. Most people recognize that when someone reveals their flaws, they usually appear more candid and honest. Remember that just because a person is "being candid and honest," you cannot know they <u>are</u> a candid and honest person. Learning that takes more time. However, when two people sit down and let each other know, in a credible way, that they are being open with each other, the trust level is raised. With an added level of trust, the conversation can easily move beyond the weather and to other subjects that are more personal or particular to why you are with the person.

It may seem the wrong move for someone giving a sales presentation to tell his prospective client that he is nervous or for someone speaking to a group of a hundred to open by saying she has butterflies. Studies show (no, I don't know which ones) that most people are terrified to speak to a group and will avoid it whenever possible. With that in mind, you can count on nearly every audience member feeling like they could never stand where the speaker is standing. They will immediately identify with any fear she professes and may be endeared by it. She could make a joke of her worries. That would allow the speaker to make her "confession" in a way that saves face while giving the audience a bit of a laugh. People love to laugh at what they fear.

For the salesperson, it can be challenging. If you tell your client you are "a bit nervous," they may wonder if that comes from your lack of confidence in your product or your company's ability to perform. The confession here must be more subtle than in other situations. It would be best to find a way to balance your need to relieve your internal pressures without engendering doubts in the client's mind. Confess a reason you might be nervous rather than being "nervous." Such as: "I am flattered that you gave me this time to speak to you. I will make sure we make the most of your time." This lets you express humility to the client and tells them you are concerned for their needs. And, by making a relatively tame statement, you may achieve a reduction of inner stress similar to saying, "I am nervous."

Many times, the nervousness comes from being in a new job. I see no detriment, in most situations, to saying to your client that you are still somewhat new, that you may not have every answer, and that you welcome the opportunity to find a solution for them. It would help if you asked for your client's input in learning about their needs and how your company can help. (of course, even someone well-seasoned should do that!) Most people like to assist the "new guy" or the "underdog." If you are sincere in using this, you will likely find more people willing to help than those who will turn you away.

Finally, for the blind date, the speaker, or the salesperson, there is something else to consider. By telling your particular audience that you are a bit nervous in a situationally appropriate manner, you are also telling them that they matter to you. You are saying that you value their opinion of you and what you are trying to accomplish. After all, if they meant nothing to you, there would be no reason to be nervous.

DIVORCE

A close friend has been in several long-term monogamous relationships but has never been married. When people ask about that, he responds, "100% of divorces begin with a marriage." Despite the joke, he is a serious man, and I am sure he has not avoided the pain of break-ups. For those of us that have been through a divorce or two, there is added legal and financial grief as we try to pick up the pieces of our lives and pack them in two suitcases.

But we move, and then we move on.

The Thing About Stuff

At one of my local watering holes, a man at the bar was talking to a woman. As I watched, this guy had his cell phone on the bar and picked it up to show the woman all its different ringtones. Granted, this was long enough ago that smartphones were a bit of a novelty, but I was perplexed that this was how he thought he would capture the attention of the woman he was talking to. As if she were a child, enamored by shiny things.

I had seen this guy in there since, and one of my friends told me he was going through a divorce after a long marriage. I instantly gave him a little more empathy as I was quite familiar with the emotional difficulty that divorce causes. Over the next couple of weeks, I would see this same man, and every time I saw him, he was either on his cell phone or holding the phone like he was expecting a call. It dawned on me that as he was experiencing

THE BOOK OF STAN

the change from "married" to "not married," he was moving into very unfamiliar territory, and the phone had become a bit of a security blanket.

For however long he had been married, he knew exactly who he was. He was Mr. X, husband of Mrs. X. This is my house, this is my car, this is my dog, this is what I do for a living. Divorce takes a lot of that away from us. Instead of being confident of being the husband of Mrs. X, he just knows he is not the husband of Mrs. X. His house may no longer be his house, his car may no longer be his car, and his dog is probably no longer his dog. Basically, all of his sense of "I am" had been impacted.

What does this leave? It leaves "This is what I do" and "This is what I have." Since his "I am" was next to nothing in his mind, all he had to talk to the woman at the bar about was what "I do" and what "I have." What did he have at the moment? A cell phone.

Undoubtedly, his ex was going through her own personal crisis of similar weight, though perhaps, with different symptoms.

Twenty-plus years ago, when I was dating regularly, one of the things I noticed when dating recently divorced women was the keeping of the marital house. I don't want this to sound too general, but many women seemed overly possessive of keeping the house - their home. It seemed like a symbol of victory over the ex or a response to other emotional reasons that had nothing to do with property value or their ability to maintain it. Houses, despite all the warm memories, are, above all, assets. Assets that will lose value if not properly kept up. And I have seen many nicely decorated houses that were close to falling apart.

During that time, I was dating a woman who got the house. Big, nice house. Big, nice yard. She loved gardening and Christmas. As gently as I could, I observed that perhaps it would be nice to do less gardening and lawn mowing and have more freedom. She gave it some thought, and in a few months, she had sold the house and bought a new, manageable townhome. She was a teacher, so she got to spend her summers traveling. She has always said it was the right move for her.

I am not saying you shouldn't keep a house. Just be realistic about it. Men and women alike should be aware that compromising their financial stability for emotional reasons can be detrimental.

The Gravity Of The Matter

For large bodies of mass like stars, planets, and moons, gravity is busy holding everything together without making much of a show of it. The only time we pay much attention to gravity is when apples fall to the ground. That and when we try to fly. As soon as we cast our arms to the sky, the struggle with gravity is felt. Oh, and when we stand on the bathroom scales.

But rocket scientists - being the rocket scientists they are - figured out what it takes to lift us straight off the ground: Rockets. The heavier the payload and the greater the distance to be traveled, the more powerful the rocket has to be. The Apollo space program used the gigantic Saturn V rocket booster to defeat gravity and propel us toward the moon. The thrust of Saturn V was so great that scientists estimated that the Earth was actually pushed out of its orbit by about a foot during liftoff. Of course, the Earth returned to its regular orbit after the rocket had reached a sufficient distance from the ground.

Divorce, or the death of a spouse, does something similar to most people. The emotional upheaval can be so intense as to push someone out of their usual "orbit" of day-to-day life. A normally sociable person may withdraw, or a typically subdued homebody type may find themselves at a bar talking to some guy about ringtones. New hairstyles, new attitudes, a new gym membership (of course), and quite often, dating many new people.

Obviously, after being divorced for a while, this person doesn't fall right back into the same old orbit... The marriage is over.

But once the emotional upheaval of a divorce begins to lessen, once that sufficient distance has been achieved, the person will likely move back towards their old normalcy, though without the spouse.

After my second divorce, I saw a counselor for a while. She told me that the gurus of the psychological field agree that after a divorce or the death of a spouse, it was close to five years before you were really ready for another marriage. I scoffed, but I began to understand as the years ticked by. In the beginning, I was way out of my orbit. I look back at my attempts at relationships and feel a bit bad that I wasn't entirely "available." I probably confused the hell out of a few people. Sorry about that.

And like with my experiences, most recently divorced people are not "themselves" for a while. Forgive the new-age cliché, but they are not yet the person they are becoming. It may vary, but in my observation, it takes about two years to stabilize and feel at ease in yourself and your new orbit. In the meantime, many people are a mess until there is enough emotional distance between them and the divorce and a new normal is found.

Emotional Gravity

While on the phone with a woman I had been to dinner with, she began talking about something going on with her ex, with whom she had a child. I can't remember all the details, but she said something that I found interesting enough to write down. She was trying to decide whether to tell him something and said, "I've already ruined his life... I guess I shouldn't ruin his day too."

We chuckled a bit, but she was serious when she said it. The divorce was her idea, and for whatever reason, a couple years later, she was still feeling guilty about it. None of this came up when we were at dinner. The day we talked, something had happened between them. It didn't bother me that we spoke about something involving the ex; when you are dating, that happens all the time. It was because of something in her voice that indicated she had unfinished business with him that made me decide I would not pursue dating her.

If you have dated much, you probably felt the same thing from others, possibly within yourself: The Gravitational Pull of Exes. Exes are like satellites in orbit around the Earth. You've got the moon... makes the tides change. Then you have satellites the size of microwaves... they do bupkis. The International Space Station doesn't mess with tides or compass points, but you can see it in the sky on some nights. Kind of big.

When they talk about an ex, or you meet one at a party or, wait for it, at a family Thanksgiving, you get a feel for their lingering influence. Sometimes you can feel your date being pulled away just a little. They won't leave your side, but that subtle arm-to-arm contact is lost for a moment... or two-ish.

If you are lucky and/or paying attention, occasionally, you can save yourself early on. A friend introduced me to a woman that I was strongly attracted to.

Smart. Check.

Articulate. Check.

Nice career. Check.

And divorced for more than two years. Check.

And she still lived with her ex. Check, please.

He lived in the basement, but we are talking about tidal influences.

And by the way, the gravitational influence of an ex isn't just there when they are still close or friendly. It can exist, and quite often does, in the form of disdain that is expressed or seething under the surface. This is, to me, more challenging to deal with since hate is often nothing more than love without hope. And what are you going to do with that?

***

All that being said, I have some advice.

To those newly single, think about moving slowly in your new life. Consider that you may want different things next week than you want right now. There is no timetable you must keep to.

To those that have been single for a while, avoid dating newly single people. You may find that you meet someone while they are just re-learning to be single, and they may change what they want or things they do right in front of your eyes. The excitement may be there, but the stability...

GIVE AND TAKE

You have likely heard someone say, "She was such a taker" or "I am too much of a giver." What do people mean by that? The totally unsatisfying answer is that it means whatever it means to that person.

"Gee, I am such a taker" are words you have probably never heard anyone say. I have never heard it, though perhaps it has been said in jest. One may call someone else a giver or a taker and may call themselves a giver, but people aren't built to think of themselves as a taker.

And that time when a friend said, "He is such a taker!" As your head snapped toward her, you thought about when she didn't offer to pay for gas on that last trip or conveniently forgot her credit card when you were out to lunch last week. And that wasn't the first time! You may look upon this friend as the worst Taker you know. And here she is, berating someone else. How dare she?

In Pros or Cons, I mentioned that anything relevant would likely also be relative. When driving, no doubt you have noticed that when someone passes you, you think about what a speed demon they are. And anyone who goes slower and gets in your way should "get off the road!". This concept illustrates the difficulty in any attempt to understand Givers and Takers. You have to have precisely the same perspective as another person to know how they see this give-and-take thing. Otherwise, you only see a situation through your lens of experience - your own Sensus Communis.

What follows is a brief primer about how we can look at and perhaps better understand Giver and Taker interactions.

The Scale

Like most personality traits, the give/take factor will vary from person to person in both type and intensity. For example, let's say Givers and Takers can be rated objectively - yeah, we can talk about that later - using a scale like the one below. The center point is neutral, with five levels each of Give and Take, from one to five.

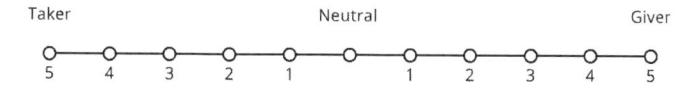

```
Taker                    Neutral                   Giver
O----O----O----O----O----O----O----O----O----O----O
5    4    3    2    1         1    2    3    4    5
```

Taker And Giver

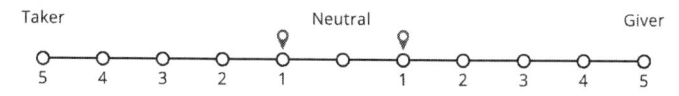

```
Taker                    Neutral                   Giver
                         ♀         ♀
O----O----O----O----O----O----O----O----O----O----O
5    4    3    2    1         1    2    3    4    5
```

In this graph, we see a Taker1 and a Giver1. They aren't that far apart and most likely get along fine when out to lunch, though there may be occasional disagreements over how much to tip the waiter. Most reasonably well-adjusted adults have learned to adapt themselves to the needs of their immediate circumstances.

Taker, Taker, And Giver

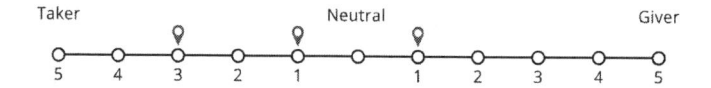

```
Taker                    Neutral                   Giver
          ♀              ♀         ♀
O----O----O----O----O----O----O----O----O----O----O
5    4    3    2    1         1    2    3    4    5
```

Then. Taker1 brings a friend to lunch that is a Taker3. After about fifteen minutes, Giver1 begins to wonder how on earth their friend can put up with this person. However, notice that Taker3 is two steps over from Taker1, just like Taker1 is two steps over from Giver1. This makes Giver1 four steps away from Taker3. Taker1 probably just rolls their eyes at things that would astound Giver1. This is where the relative side of things is more pronounced. The further away from your standard someone is, the more noticeable and perhaps offensive it is for you.

Neutral

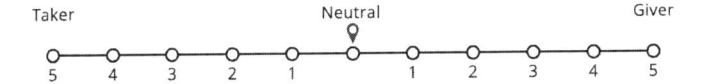

```
Taker                         Neutral                          Giver
 O——O——O——O——O——O——O——O——O——O——O
 5   4   3   2   1       1   2   3   4   5
```

By neutral, I mean someone who is well-balanced, self-sufficient, and accepts responsibility for themselves. A neutral doesn't want your money and doesn't really want or need your approval either. They will likely get a separate check, so they don't have to barter to leave the restaurant.

The Extremes

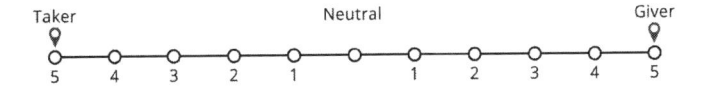

```
Taker                         Neutral                          Giver
 O——O——O——O——O——O——O——O——O——O——O
 5   4   3   2   1       1   2   3   4   5
```

So... these 5s. What are we going to do with them? It seems they could both be pathological. The only thing positive you can say about Giver5 is that they don't physically take from other people. But besides being destructive to themselves, they are disruptive to others. They are the ones that always give the most expensive present at a small birthday gathering, and they will go into debt to do it, all while skewing the standards for others. Regardless of the "no more than" budget your group sets for gifts, this person always spends over the limit and makes sure you know about it.

On the other end of the spectrum, the Taker5 is noticeable in their consumption of other people. The concept of their "fair portion" never occurs to them because they believe they deserve all they can take. This is the realm of sociopaths. To them, a Taker4.9 is just another Giver, like every other person they encounter.

◆ ◆ ◆

So, with a different slant, let's look at this set again: Giver1, Taker1, and Taker3. You dated Taker1 for a while. Though you had some good times, you felt your needs deserved more priority, and Taker1 never would do the things you preferred. Then Taker1 starts dating Taker3, and just like that, Taker1 is doing everything you always wanted them to do with you. And being a puppy dog about it. It is relative. The Alpha in one relationship can be the Beta in another.

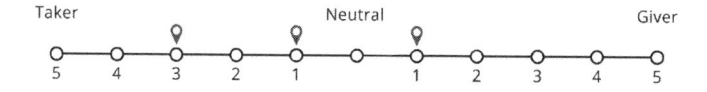

```
     Taker              Neutral              Giver
                 ♀         ♀     ♀
       O—O—O—O—O—O—O—O—O—O
       5  4  3  2  1     1  2  3  4  5
```

We deal with real people in real life, and things can get murky. I was in a relationship where I was putting my all into it, and, to me, I was the Giver, and she was the Taker. After we ended the romance, we maintained a friendship. I was Alpha and a bit of a Taker, maybe Neutral when we got together. We eventually ended up both being Neutral. Balance is much easier to achieve when there is nothing to lose for both parties.

Except for those 5s, who act compulsively, the rest of us move around a little on the scale, depending on the circumstances. A commanding and driven person in business may be an absolute pushover in a relationship. Someone who may be a Taker in romantic relationships may be a Giver with their family. It may be that we all need several graphs for the several parts of our lives where a distinction could be made.

I used the "friends at lunch" scenario rather than a dating relationship because I think the dynamics are easier to present. You can easily apply these concepts to how similar circumstances have arisen in past relationships. You may try to recognize these traits within your social group, attempt to make your own scale, and then begin to understand more about your group dynamics.

***

I have been in, observed, or talked to others about many relationships where the give/take comes into play. In the "wild," where the Givers and Takers are wandering around in the same space and bump into each other, it seems the chemical reactions go something like this:

Situation

Taker4 Meets another Taker4 at a party - They both say hello to each other. After eying each other for only a moment, they both walk away without another word.

Giver4 meets another Giver4 at the same party - they introduce themselves, ask how the other one knows the host/hostess; the weather; a polite "excuse me," and one or both sees someone else they need to talk to.

Taker4 meets Giver4 at the party - Giver4 introduces themselves, and Taker4 responds. They have sex in the bathroom. A torrid six-week affair ensues. They break up.

Cont'd.

Breakdown

The Takers

The Takers don't want anything to do with each other because they know they can't get anything from the other.

The Taker and the Giver

The Taker and the Giver hit it off immediately because the Giver immediately starts trying to give, and the Taker immediately starts taking what the Giver is giving. The Giver, feeling appreciated, gives more. The Taker naturally takes all the Giver can give. The Giver "has never felt this way" and is so satisfied that he/she has found someone with whom they have a genuine connection. However, a Giver doesn't just want to give love; they want it in return.

To begin with, the Giver's senses are overwhelmed by the newness of it all. Somewhere along the way, the Taker is going to say, in so many words, "I love the way you give to me." when the Giver was expecting, "Thank you. Here is something for you." That is about the time the Giver looks at his/her cookie jar and sees it is almost empty, while the Taker's cookie jar is so full that it is overflowing. It's a metaphor.

Realizing the now obvious imbalance, the Giver decides it is time to hold on to those cookies until the Taker gives up some of theirs. The Taker, oblivious to anything other than not getting more cookies, says, "You've changed." You know what happens next.

The Givers

When a Giver is with another Giver, one gives, and the other gives back, but they don't feel they have given of themselves when everything is even. They must see the number of cookies in the jar go down to allow themselves to feel they are now worthy of love in return. Unless two Givers of similar intensity are self-aware enough to know what is going on in their heads, they are unlikely to stay together. This is because they both will feel unworthy of the other's attention. Ironically, they <u>are</u> the ones worthy of the other's attention and don't realize it.

And...

This is an oversimplification, but the Neutral will give you their cookie if they want to, not because they have to.

As with all things non-hallucinogenic... reality is the boss. Use these concepts to help guide your expectations, but please don't think someone will change from what they are. The Ghost of Christmas Past will not visit. You should always plan on getting your own turkey. The Neutrals already have theirs.

Oh... I mentioned "fair" earlier. Years ago, a business partner and I met with a lawyer, and my partner said that he thought something the other side wanted wasn't fair. The lawyer told us how an old professor of his handled fairness. He said, "Fair is what you agree to."

There is no "the way it is supposed to be" in dating or most of life. As discussed in The Irwinian Theorem > The Formula, if your expectations are out of line with your experience, you are heading for disappointment. So, that last relationship... did they Take, or did they just not Give what you wanted?

COMPUTER DATING AD TERMINOLOGY*

I used to look at computer dating ads occasionally and have made a few stories out of them and have a few observations. Granted, we all think and act based on our own experiences and interpretations. Still, I would like to provide guidance on what some standard terms and keywords used in this medium actually mean.

I yield to the new-age concept that you are successful if you feel successful; you are beautiful in your own way; you are intelligent in your own right... you are worthy.

Notwithstanding your self-realization, I offer the following:

1. "Athletic"

Girls and Guys, I realize that a Sumo wrestler is considered an athlete... but, come on, that is not what "Body type: Athletic" means to most people. And you don't qualify for "Athletic" just because you played thirty minutes of basketball with the guys last Thursday night or because you walked your Bichon Frise to the mailbox twice in one day.

If that is the case, then I am beyond slender. Let's see now... my shoulders are athletic, my legs are above average, and my head is slim, but let's not talk about my waist. Have you seen any good movies lately?

2. "Prefer Not To Say"

Girls, are you hiding out from the FBI or what?

This is a fascinating response to the "Have Children:" line. Tell me... do you think no one will notice the playpen or the tween pop-diva posters in the other bedroom?

Or the response line for "Religion?" When I see "Rather Not Say" on this line, the first thing that comes to mind is something that involves human sacrifice.

"Smoking: Prefer Not To Say"... Hmm, let me guess.

You usually see two or three of these in the same ad that also says, "Must be open and honest."

3. "Successful"

Guys, this usually does not mean that you finally passed your GED or could pay off the new chrome wheels on your 1970s muscle car. Most people view this as having reached a financial level of security. Like, you have your own house, and it is in a neighborhood where you don't have to have bars on the windows. Well... wait a minute, that would exclude some pretty swanky areas. Okay. You can have bars on your windows if you actually have something inside the house worth stealing... but not car parts. Yeah. That's it.

4. "Must be honest!"

This is usually a woman telling everyone that she always picks lying bums. She doesn't realize that by saying this, she is telling the next lying bum that she is vulnerable to his ways. Think about it. An honest person is going to be honest. A dishonest person is going to be dishonest. Therefore, every person you ask, "Are you honest?" will say "Yes."

Girls, really watch out for a guy that asks for honesty.

5. "Sensitive"

Guys, this is not a word found on a condom package. It does not attach itself to phrases like, "Yeah baby... right there."

It doesn't mean you smile and laugh whenever you see a puppy or cry whenever someone mentions that baby seal season is open. The words for that are Manic Depressive.

It means that you pay attention to her. That you are aware of her wants, needs, and desires... without her saying a word. It means that you mention her new haircut before she does. It means you can read her every feeling from the way she breathes. It means you already know without her saying.

6. "Celebrity you look like?"

No... I am sorry, you don't.

7. "Wanted: Man for a casual or serious relationship."

Ladies. There may be a fatal flaw in the wording here. Just remember, you said it. Don't go whining and crying or blaming all the rest of us men when you find out he chose "Casual."

8. "No Preference"

Guys. What are you saying when you answer "No Preference" to every question in the area that describes what you want in a woman? And, give a height range of 4' to 6' and an age span that covers three decades? You are not saying you have no preference; you are saying you don't care. You are either saying that you don't know yourself well enough to know what you want, or you just want to get laid. And don't ask me what my point is.

9. "Must like cats!"

Okay. There really aren't any men that match the rest of what you are asking for, and also - like cats. This is a truth about men, quite similar to leaving the toilet seat up. We will put up with the cats for you because we are attracted to you. The only animals men want on their kitchen counters are filleted, soaking in bourbon, and waiting to hit the grill. And NO, it isn't cute how the cat jumps into bed with you. If you notice this "cat lover" nodding off during the conversation, he probably took antihistamines before coming to your place, so he wouldn't sneeze from all the damn cat hair floating everywhere. Next time he comes over... look in his glove compartment. I guarantee there will be a lint roller in there. When he leaves and turns the corner, he is probably rolling everything... including his teeth.

10. "Must like dogs!"

Okay.

11. Spelling/Grammatical Usage

Please... Please pay attention. I don't claim to be the guru of grammar. I was of a certain age before I finally got the Who/Whom thing straight. But these just kill me:

Your - You're -
"Your" denotes possession, as in, "Your car is nice."
"You're" is a contraction of the words "you are," as in, "You're going to the store with me."
They can properly be used in the same sentence, "You're going to let me drive your car, aren't you?"

There - They're - Their - Okay... double close attention.
"There" denotes a location, as in, "He is over there."
"They're" is a contraction of the words "they are," as in "They're in the kitchen."

"Their" denotes possession, as in, "Their car was stolen."
And, believe it or not, all three can be used in one sentence, as with, "They're going to park their car over there."

General - if you try to be clever and write beyond your average conversational level... learn that the Spell Checker is your friend. Trust it. Consult with it.

Of course, this is just some advice from an outside observer. Do with it what you will.

COMPUTER AD REPLY

The Ad:

About me:

Seeking: Long Term Relationship

Religion: None/Agnostic/Don't Care

Education: Graduate

Employment: Full Time

Profile: Athletic/Fit - 5 ft 6 in - Non-smoker - Occasional drinker - No children

Interests: Arts & Crafts-Community Service-Movies-Music-Outdoor Activities-Theater

About you :

"You are me, i.e., over-educated, well-read, diverse interests, nurturing, a comedian, come up with the worst p-u puns, attractive, attentive, and ready to just jump in and get your hair wet."

The Reply:

Howdy, ma'am... I couldn't help but notice your ad in these personals. I see you already prefer a guy named "i.e." cause you said, "You are me, i.e." Well, my name is Bob... Bob Johnson...

so I hope that ain't too far off base for you. Just like you said, I am over bein' educated cause, like you, I am a graduate. I have diverse interests since I can work on carburetors and transmissions. I did give up nurturing when I was pretty young, though, when my momma weaned me.

I don't know why you want to be a comedian... you'd just be laughing and cuttin' up all the time and probably have one of those athletic fits you were talkin' about... then you would need an occasional drink to calm down. But... like you, I say NO children when you are having a drink... that young, they just don't know when to quit, and then there ain't enough liquor left for me. It's good that you don't smoke cause that way, I don't have to hide my Marlboro's like I do the bourbon.

It's a shame about that stutter when you write "p-u puns,"... but that was the only place in the whole letter where it came up. Seems like you got it under control and all.

I see you are interested in Community Service and Outdoor Activities. My last community service was outdoors too. The judge said he had never seen such a good job of cleaning up a right-of-way, and he got me to do his back yard too.

Usually, when I jump in the water, I get more than my hair wet... but I guess if you can do it, I'll give it a go too. I am seeking a Long-Term-Relationship just like you. So, as long as I can be back to the garage by 7:00 am on Monday, I think we got a deal.

Just one more thing... under religion, I see that you are a None. I got nothing against Catholics; I just don't want to have to eat fish on Friday. What say we travel on down to the theater and see one of those movies you like? Elvis is my favorite, and he makes music too.

Your new beau - Bob

PS - since you got a job and all... can you pay for the movie?

AN INDEPENDENT WOMAN

In a couple of decades of being single many a date looked me right in the eye and, almost as a preemptive strike, said, "I am a <u>very</u> independent woman." To which I would typically reply, "Are you 'independent' or 'anti-dependent'?" Some got what I was saying and responded, often with a smirky smile, that they may be a "touch anti-dependent." Some seemed at a genuine loss about what I was asking. Some just growled.

What can I say? I am a witty conversationalist.

For those who don't have smirky smiles on their face, I will elaborate.

Genuinely independent people don't even notice their independence… they just ARE. However, some are so dependent on what others think, or to make a point, they must somehow prove or announce their "independence."

Granted, sometimes, that independence was recent and perhaps came out of difficulties that would not soon be forgotten. In those cases, it may seem like the thing to say, but too much focus on what should be a strength can reveal a weakness. The message sent is that you are not confident in your "self" and must keep people at arm's length.

That's all there really is to say on this one.

S.O.U.P.

When you first get into a relationship, it is easy to let things just happen without giving them much thought. It is an exciting time for most. Getting to know each other, especially if there is a physical and emotional connection, can keep you in a state of elation. You know you are deeply distracted by a relationship when your friends tap you on the head and ask if anybody's home. And, frequently, you aren't home. Your mind is with that other person, wondering what they are doing, looking forward to the next time you're together.

That newness is like a jet taking off from a runway, probably out of Atlanta, climbing higher and higher, seeming like it will never end. But it hits 30,000 or 40,000 feet, otherwise known as 'cruising altitude,' and levels out. Not bad, though. You are flying high and fast, and they let you take your seatbelt off. Easy peasy.

Somehow, as your mind takes in this blissful moment, you are able to break the loving gaze you are sharing long enough to look out the window at all that is passing beneath. The Grand Canyon is lovely from up here... Wait a minute! As your head snaps back to the startled look of your new love, you say, "Aren't we going to Vermont?" At about that time, the masks drop from the ceiling above you.

Why? Because all the oxygen is sucked out of the room as you utter the words that have taken many a relationship from 30,000 feet to almost scraping the treetops: "Where is this relationship going?"

Pardon the abrupt change in metaphor, but in the 1920s, there was a physicist named Heisenberg. He was a heavy hitter in the quantum particle side of physics and published what is now known as Heisenberg's Uncertainty Principle. In the subatomic world, particles bounce around all over the place, and compared to full-sized life, they are moving at incredible speeds. For experiments, physicists often have to look at position and velocity. Roughly - where is it, and how fast is it going in a particular direction? The Uncertainty Principle proposes that the more you try to define specifically "where" a particle is, the less you can know about its velocity. And, the more you focus on velocity, the less you know "where" the particle is.

Isn't that the way with relationships? Things click at the start of a new relationship, and we are climbing fast and "headed thataway." And, like the couple at the beginning, you have likely been in a relationship where you were enjoying the trip until you realized your significant other (SO) wasn't headed in the same direction as you. You were, seemingly, in sync in the beginning and had only been concerned with the fact that you were moving, not the "where" you were as a couple. And, like those little particles, you can't be certain where you are in the relationship while flying along at speed.

And, since you have likely had one of those "Where is this relationship going?" conversations, you have experienced firsthand that feeling that you aren't moving at all. That feeling you are, floating, stuck right in that place, until the "we need to talk" has worn off and you are moving again. It looks like, pun intended, you are in the S.O.U.P., AKA, under the influence of the **Significant Other Uncertainty Principle**. All you wanted to know was "where," you didn't want to stop the plane.

Like the other uncertainty principle, S.O.U.P doesn't come into play if you aren't trying to measure or define anything. You just keep doing what you are doing. Speed usually only comes up if you and your SO differ substantially. What can trip you up is "Where are we?" and "Where are we going?" If you ask your SO, "Where are we headed?" and the response is "Thataway," to which you say, "Cool," velocity doesn't have to change. However, if you don't like the answer or want to talk about "where we are," then that requires both of you to focus on the "measurement" process.

In this "relationship reset" phase, the uncertainty is greatest. Work, travel, family pressures, or the like may have brought it on. Perhaps one of the parties has been through a significant life event, such as a new job or the loss of a loved one. These are all reasonable, relatable things that people go through.

You set aside speed and direction while you figure out what was causing that feeling of uncertainty. If the concerns of both of you are allayed, you may start anew, perhaps on an even better path. Solving a problem together can bring more closeness.

Of course, a different outcome may be that the relationship ends after the first talk or some subsequent time. Sometimes, relationships run their course, and emotionally intelligent people should be willing to recognize when it is time to move on.

There are many ways the S.O.U.P. can affect a relationship. None of us like uncertainty. But which is worse, the uncertainty of asking a question, the answer to which you may not like?... Or, metaphorically, ending up in California instead of Vermont.

.

OVERLOAD

Have you ever been in an "on-again/off-again" relationship that you just couldn't end?

Hold that thought.

When I was about 15, I decided I needed a strobe light. It was the very late 60s, but it was the 60s nonetheless. As the son of an electrician, I had grown up working with circuits and knew that if I could make and break the connection (ON/OFF) at a decent rate, I could get the right effect from a light bulb. I didn't want to flip a switch back and forth, so I had to devise an alternate method.

I had a record player that would spin the platter at three different speeds, and the record platter was made of metal. All I had to do was place electrical tape at equal spacing on the metal, then rig an electrical contact that would touch the metal except when the electrical tape passed under the connection. As the platter turned, the circuit would make and break like a switch turning on and off. Then I could wire this to a light bulb and plug it into the wall and - PRESTO - a flashing light that would mimic the operation of an actual strobe, with three speeds!

The basics were correct, but I was unaware of a particular aspect of electrical power. A 60-watt light bulb draws very little amperage on a 120-volt circuit... unless you turn it on and off a lot. Like, if you are using it as a strobe light. When you do that, it creates a load on the circuit roughly equating... give or take...

guessing here, a two thousand-watt light bulb. And this while using a simple lamp cord for power.

Well, that plain old everyday lamp cord I had plugged into the wall heated up and disintegrated in a flash, leaving an interesting burn mark on the hardwood floors and a smoke-filled room from the burning insulation. I still contemplate the long-term effects of that smoke at times. Though I never researched the technical term that applied to what happened, I had no trouble spontaneously thinking of a couple of non-technical terms that suited the moment. When the smoke cleared, no pun intended, I realized that I had overloaded the capacity of the lamp cord, causing it to fail.

Back to the beginning. Have you ever been in an on-again/off-again relationship? I will answer that for you. If you have been in many relationships, you have. A psychiatrist may say I am "projecting" my failures onto others. The possibility of projection notwithstanding, I readily admit that I have been in more than one.

Say, you are in a relationship where you appreciate aspects of it... companionship, sex, or whatever. But you know the relationship isn't going anywhere, and you may even know you shouldn't have started it in the first place. So, you are sitting alone at home one evening, and you say to yourself, "I really should end this." And you do.

If you do this when you should, it usually ends up with you both telling each other that you both agree on the split, had a great time, and will remain friends. You don't have to raise your voice, tell each other mean things, and you don't run the person down to your friends. You just say it wasn't working out, and you move along.

Two weeks later...

So, you are sitting alone at home one evening, and you say to yourself, "It wasn't that bad. We had a great time together. I really liked the sex. I miss them. I should call." And you do.

And, it turns out, they are feeling the same thing. You get a drink together, you enjoy each other's company, you have sex, and you have breakfast. And, in a flash, everything is back to normal. But, if everything is back to normal, then nothing has changed. Whether the timing is days, weeks, or months, you realize that the same things that made you decide to break up the first time are still there, but this time you resent them a little more. You may even accept that you messed up and you own the resentment.

You talk. This time the resentment has a seat at the table... for both of you. A few grievances are aired on both sides, both voices have a strained "I need to be heard" quality, emotions run a little hot, and you and your resentment walk out the door.

Four weeks later...

I won't do the details because we all know what happens next. With each reunion and breakup, there are more grievances, more strained voices, and more heated emotions. It seems a cycle that you cannot escape until one day, the real overload happens.

Grievances are fully aired, strained words that are definitely heard, and then the finale. The buildup of heat reaches the combustion point, with smoke in the air and scorch marks on the floor. And two otherwise lovely people walk away from each other, often bitter and rarely wiser.

I can't tell you how to break the cycle, but I can tell you what happens if you don't.

WHY DO MEN? PART I

The Problem With Decades

Note: This likely applies more to people over 50-something.

Female friends often ask me, "Why do men act that way?" or "Why do men seem like they don't know what they're doing?" One response I have offered for such a question is that men often don't know what decade a woman is from. I don't mean when she was born, but the decade that has the most influence over her current thought processes.

When I was a kid in the early 60s, the idea that the woman's place was in the home was, for most, the standard. In the late 60s and through the 70s, women became more liberated. After a few years of merely enjoying a more open sexual lifestyle, men became confused.

The woman of the 80s really began to take her place in business. Well-educated, highly motivated women were climbing the corporate ladder, beating their male counterparts at sales, and starting new companies at a brisk pace. In the 90s, women found themselves attaining more and more equality, and men found themselves in less and less control.

During these 40-plus years of change, it seems that some women who are very modern in their business ways often remain more traditional in their relationship attitudes. She might be an 80s woman in business and a 50s or 60s woman in a relationship. She may be a 90s woman in a relationship, taking control and having high expectations of a man's consideration of her in every respect, yet is not motivated toward a career life at all.

Our attraction to people is often influenced, if not based on, our initial impression of that person. So, when a man dates someone with whom his first contact was as an assertive, confident businesswoman, he may be disappointed that she is very mild-mannered and passive in a relationship. Or, he may be perfectly happy with it. Or vice versa on all that. Hence, my statement that the man may be confused as to which "decade" the woman he's dating is most attuned.

Not saying that anyone is right or wrong, just that this is one more spot where relationships between people of a certain age can hit a bump in the road.

WHY DO MEN? PART II

The Problem With Now

Continuing with the theme from Part I on "Why do men act like that?" If you find yourself asking that question, perhaps you should first ask yourself what makes you think they should do something different. In other words, what is the basis for your expectation in this particular circumstance?

This question seems to come up a lot related to when a man and woman meet in a bar and chat for a while, exchange numbers, and agree to talk "soon," but the follow-up never happens. We should avoid getting so caught up with what transpires in a casual setting that we treat it with more weight than it deserves. If someone misleads another about their intentions on purpose, they should be held accountable. But let's set aside those rapscallion types.

Regular, sociable, sincere people - both men and women - can be out and meet someone they talk with for a while and find themselves attracted to "in the moment." Loose plans may be discussed, numbers provided, etc., and no follow-through happens.

Alcohol often plays a part in such exchanges, but not necessarily. Sometimes it is just the difference between PM and AM. In the cold light of day, we remind ourselves why we don't want to get involved, why this isn't a good time, or whatever reasoning seems to fit. It wasn't that he or she was being deceitful last night. Either party may have been polite in asking or merely non-confrontational when accepting.

When something like this happens, you shouldn't miss a beat. Don't even wonder, "What did I do wrong?" Don't let your expectations get ahead of your experience. Feel free to engage the next time a similar opportunity arises and have a good time.

GOOD QUESTION

A friend and I exchanged emails, and she asked, "Do you think I was so comfortable with new Bob because he was just like old Bob, my ex? The outward trappings were not the same. Superficial likes and dislikes were different also. But maybe, the core person was very, very similar."

I replied, "The Irwinian Theorem maintains that deep-level attraction is entirely subliminal and, therefore, uncontrollable on a conscious level."

This brought about further conversation about what attracts us to others, which I have tried to round out for general consumption. (Just trying to be thoughtful.)

◆ ◆ ◆

Sure, you can look at people and see they have the typical features of a "good-looking" person, but what makes you pick good-looking person A over good-looking person B?

In Zebra Stripes, I offered the idea that our attractions are greatly influenced, if not governed, by the bonding that occurs with others just after birth. This pushes us to be subconsciously attracted to people we perceive to be a suitable match for the "zebra stripe" imprint in our minds. And often, we don't know what we are being attracted to until thoughts of "I did it again" present themselves.

In my experience, the response to that subliminal attraction can become increasingly conscious with the knowledge and acceptance that the whole subconscious scenario exists. The more you maintain this conscious awareness, the sooner it comes front of mind when meeting someone new until you almost immediately know what is driving the attraction forward. Much better to have an "aha!" moment than an "uh-oh" one.

The real challenge for me has not been the realization of being in the danger zone but exercising the good sense to walk away when I know I am in it. It is as if a small voice within says, "Go ahead... since you know what it is, you can control it." All I end up doing is reliving the same event, but with even more frustration because I am "fully aware" that I am being stupid since I have lost my "ignorance is bliss" status. Does that make sense?

The goal is 1) to bring the unconscious feelings/actions to the surface so they become conscious. Then 2) take the right course of action and not make decisions based on pre-programmed zombie-like reactions but on knowing what is right and best for you. Acting completely "in the present" can be challenging and takes determination and practice. Practice that typically comes with failures that reinforce the correctness of "staying awake."

Now, the million-dollar question (in multiple parts).

- Is the other person the way they are because of how we are?

- Are we the way we are because we are triggered by another person to react in a pre-determined pattern rather than act the way we would like?

- If two people that would typically evoke pre-determined patterns in each other were totally conscious of that tendency, would/could they stay "in the present" long enough to learn to live "in the present" together?

Accepting the answer to the third point is "yes"; regardless of how conscious and in the moment you are, you have to put yourself in front of other people, probably many others, to find someone that can mesh with you on that level.

It took Edison thousands of tries to find a filament that would make a light bulb last long enough for practical use… but they all gave some light. He had to wonder… each time he saw the glow… is this the one?

ONE

Full moonlight falls at his feet
Broken as it passes through a wintered tree
Still shimmering white against the night
Lays bright upon what would otherwise be unknown

Soft music breaks the silent still
Notes that cause the heart to hold a beat
And make breath stand motionless in air,
Come to be as both salt and salve

This space beside… still a space
Can only share its vacant stare
Would it calm a soul were it to dance
With moonlight, melody, and he

SECTION III: HUMOR

How do you introduce a section on humor? I am afraid to make jokes, so as not to spoil any of what is to follow. Having been single for just about thirty years at this writing, I have spent a lot of time alone. Which means that you often have to laugh at yourself since no one is close by to help enjoy life's moments.

Over the years I have gotten good at that – having moments, that is. And I write a lot of them down - yes, type. Out of respect for those of sensitive disposition I have left some hilarious stuff out of this section. You will just have to trust me on that. And, hopefully, I have left some mildly humorous events here to share.

Enough dawdling.

THE BATHROOM*

Guys, you have probably dealt with this if you have been married or have lived with a woman for a while. The bathroom and the female occupation thereof. It isn't anything new or unique. Everyone has been there. Dashing leading men of the movies regularly walk into bathrooms with stockings hanging from everything something can hang from. Henry VIII would have only married a couple of times if his wives had stayed out of his way in the bathroom. If Anne Boleyn had only known.

You don't understand if you have just gone away with her for a weekend or two. You think the bathroom was that way because she was out of her usual environment, unfamiliar circumstances, packing concerns, and time constraints. That's right, that's all it is. You go right ahead thinking it won't be that way later. And don't ever fall for the "There aren't enough drawers!" story. The Archimedes Principle of Relationships states that every drawer you empty will immediately fill back up with stuff you didn't even know she had.

When you are young and early on in your first live-in relationship, you are interested in - even somewhat fascinated by - the Getting Ready process. After all, you have nothing else to do since you are ready in ten minutes and have so much time to kill you could watch a pay-per-view. But, out of loving respect, you stand in the doorway and make conversation... all the while wondering why she has to hold her mouth that way while putting on eye shadow. I mean, at least when we shave, we have to keep our mouths that way to get all the stubble. Then, like the tenderfoot rookie that you are,

You ask:	What does this do?
She says:	It takes the oil off of my face.
You ask:	And what does that do?
She says:	It puts the oil back.
You ask:	Why do you do that?
She says:	You wouldn't understand.
You shut up:	You are learning.

Later, there comes the day when you are at the sink and look down to see a little black speck of something on the counter. In an unusually tidy moment, you think to yourself, "Hey. I'll clean that little speck off the counter." Proudly you reach down... unaware that you are about to unleash a power that nuclear fission specialists don't understand. The Mascara Speck. Einstein said the Mascara Speck is the most mysteriously self-replicating compound known to man. One touch of the finger creates a black streak on the counter roughly the size of the bottom of a jar of moisturizer.

So you put the moisturizer jar on top of the streak to cover it up.

In another unusually tidy (though guilt-driven) moment, you move the jar to finish cleaning up the mark. When you move the jar, the bottom slides across the mark, making it even more prominent. You try to clean up with your finger again, and now the mark is growing exponentially.

It takes three gallons of paint to redo your bedroom, but you can recolor the entire house with one mascara speck. Every jar on the counter now has the "black plague" on the bottom, and each shift of the jars to clean one spot creates more black marks until your entire bathroom looks like the La Brea tar pit.

In a desperate search for some device or solution to help end this and clean the bathroom before "she" comes in... you open a cabinet door. Under the sink is the graveyard for all the beauty gizmos that were absolute necessities for about... oh... five days. The fingernail polish dryer; the steam set hair curlers; and, oh yeah, the Home Electrolysis Kit. That was interesting until she decided your offers to help were motivated by the pure torture that electrolysis induces.

Hey... look... a sponge. Oops!! No, can't use those sponges.

What the hell! You decide to use a dry towel, so you use one that is handy and it works pretty well. Within a few minutes, you finally get the countertop back in order. Exhausted from cleaning up the mascara, you flop down on the toilet. Thank God your significant other has taught you how to put the toilet seat down, or you would have fallen in.

At about that time, she walks into the bathroom. "Honey, thanks for straightening up the counter. It looks great. Hey, have you seen a towel that I had here? It is part of a monogrammed set I am giving Mom and Dad at their anniversary party tonight."

Don't move. Maybe she won't see you.

I used to date a woman that got on to me about the toilet seat. To be polite while at her house, I became more conscious about putting the seat and the lid back down. Then she told me I should just put the seat down and leave the top up. Wait a minute now. I understood that putting it all down made the bathroom look neat and orderly, but I didn't understand her new request. She told me it was how it was "supposed" to be - seat down, lid up. I shut up. I had already learned.

AISLE 17

I was at MY grocery store today. Nearly everyone says, "My <fill in the blank>" whenever they refer to the grocery store where they shop. I don't know why we would feel so attached to a grocery store that we would address it in such a possessive manner. I suppose that even though we do not have to farm and hunt for our food, we still must form some sort of bond with the entity that handles that for us.

Several years ago, I wondered why that bond remained strong at MY store. All evidence was that the corporates just gave up in my neighborhood. The leading competitor had moved in up the street, and MY store had been going downhill ever since. I can't tell you how many times I meant to write those guys and tell them to snap out of it. Spruce this place up a little! But, enough about feeling abandoned by your grocery store. The corporates had heard my telepathic message and had begun a significant facelift to the store. A new entrance, a new ceiling line, new shelving, and a new tile floor. Fresh!

One of the things that happened when they replaced the floor tiles and shelving was the "shuffle." They must move everything from aisles 2 and 3 to aisles 17 and 18 so that they can replace the shelving racks. It would have been okay if they had actually moved everything from aisles 2 and 3 to aisles 17 and 18. In mid-shuffle, nobody knew where anything was.

The incredible thing was this. It became fun to go to the store. It was like a scavenger hunt. Everyone was walking up and down aisles with humorously lost looks on their faces. On one trip, I picked out some cheese and headed to get some crackers. A day and a half later, I found the crackers on aisle 17, ten feet from the cheese. While on my quest for the perfect cracker, I picked up several other sojourners on a common search. We had a campfire and sang songs. One fellow told the story of when he spread peanut butter all over a saltine, and it didn't even break. There was admiration in every eye.

One day I was there and wanted to pick up some salmon. As I headed down the aisle to the fish counter, I noticed that everything from aisle 10 was on aisle 1. This re-shuffle meant that the wine was crammed right next to the bread. It seemed logical to me, but there was a problem. The aisle was so narrow that you couldn't pull out a loaf of bread without bumping into the wine bottles. It was a real dilemma for the Baptist shoppers, but some Catholics were having communion.

As I went down the aisle, a woman stood there - that same lost look in her eyes, just looking around in circles. Half smiling, she looked at me as I approached and said, "I just don't know where anything is!" Now that I think about it, maybe she had done more than just "bumping into" the wine bottles. Screw-tops are our friends when in the wild.

Consider this, though. Everybody drives home the same way they do every day. They stop at the store and pick up milk and bread like always. But not then. During the shuffle, they had to look for it. What a change of pace from the predictable, follow-the-pattern, trip home. Now we have an adventure. I know there is probably some husband that just proudly hunted down a can of stewed tomatoes that will go home with a smile on his face - and his wife will wonder what the hell he is up to. "Hanging out in frozen foods again, honey?"

Back then, it struck me as I walked away that in the last few times I had been to MY store - since the aisle shifts had begun - several people had just struck up conversations with me (or I, them) about being a little bewildered. At the fish counter, the clerk told me about a woman who said she had started buying different things than usual because she had to look around instead of going straight to the same-old shelf.

It was causing people to talk to each other, break out of the rut, and make things unpredictable. And in turn, people started to look to others for reassurance and help. A clinical psychologist could do an entirely new study on the phenomenon.

I had found the answer to complacency in America. Every three or four months, play musical aisles in the grocery stores. Change everything around. Don't make it so easy on us. Keep us guessing. Make us forage for our food, and we will regain the primordial satisfaction of self-sufficiency.

Hey. Isn't it double coupon day?

YOU CAN'T BE TALKING ABOUT ME!

More than once, I have been asked if I "have been like this for a long time?" In varying circumstances, I pretend I don't know what the question means, but for the most part, I do. "Exactly how long have you been a smart-ass?" First, let me say that I would much rather be a smart-ass than a dumb-ass. Second. How or when I developed a propensity for taking advantage of someone's lack of preparedness is unknown. My mother would say it was all those MAD Magazines in the late sixties. I discovered early in life it wasn't always what you said directly that pushed a bamboo shoot under someone's fingernail. It was often a subtle response... the non-verbal communication of "Nah, Nah, Nah" that really gets to people.

In 1970 and 1972, I had a part-time summer job working for the State of Georgia as a painter. The State Building Authority needed a lot of work done that was "beneath" a real painter, so they hired quite a few of their regular employees' sons to do the job. My father was an electrician for the State, so I was on the crew.

In 1972 the crew painted parking decks for a couple of weeks and then a large wrought iron fence around the Governor's mansion. After that, it was time for the vital work of the summer. The State Capitol. If you know the Georgia State Capitol, it has a beautiful dome covered with real gold that was mined in the mountains of north Georgia. Below the gold dome, the roof of the main part of the building was made of aluminum sheeting called "standing seam." This part of the Capitol roof was prone to leaking when a good rain came along. To seal the roof, it was necessary to "paint" it with a gloppy thick specialized paint. This paint was designed to seal up anything it came in contact with. It was an "aluminized" paint, meaning it had a lot of aluminum to help accomplish... well, I don't know what the aluminum did. I do know that when it dried, it was green and gleaming from the flecks of aluminum in the mixture.

Bob was our "adult supervision" for the summer. He had been a painter for the Building Authority for quite some time, and I am sure he did not relish the idea of being our nursemaid. For some reason, our painting with this thick goo-ey paint gave him a gleam in his eye. It didn't take any skill to apply. Mostly, you slopped it on the roof, which was the floor to us, with a roller, and the job was done. One day we were working on the walls along the sides of the building... some above our heads. That day, Bob told us why he was laughing while we painted. "Boys, y'all be careful 'cause if you get that paint in your pretty long hair (remember, it was 1972), it won't come out, and tomorrow you'll come in with a new haircut. Heh, heh." I guess no one had ever been able to get the paint out once it was in.

Yes... it happened. I moved to the left as the guy beside me moved to the right. A big glop of this paint landed right on my head. Bob was ecstatic. "Well, Bailey. Looks like mommy's gonna have the scissors out tonight." My hair wasn't very long - pretty conservative by some standards - but I was determined not to lose any of it (I wish I could say that now). I certainly didn't want to give Bob the pleasure that he looked forward to the next day. I rode home from work with my father, who also got a bit of a kick out of my predicament. I had a dried brick in my hair, and on the way home, I started twisting, squeezing, and pulling... trying my best to separate the big block into smaller pieces.

I spent about three hours working on my hair that night. I was finally able to pull a comb through it. Sweet victory. I hadn't lost a strand... well, at least I hadn't lost a patch. On the other hand, a large portion of my hair was shiny green (I was years before my time). A painter's hat concealed my success the following day. Bob had fun talking about the "bald" spot I must be covering. When I took the hat off, he was speechless, and the fun and games were over. He sneered as he said, "Time for work." Several times I got that look that said, "You just think you're somethin', don't ya, smart boy?" Amazing how some victories can be so sweet. And amazingly enough, not the last time I got that look.

Though I never got more of that paint in my hair, we all got a good portion of it on our shoes and clothes. Like my hair that day, we all had a nice shiny green look for weeks.

There was a snack bar on the building's first floor, and we took our morning breaks there daily. The same girl worked the cash register each day, and she finally asked what we were doing. I told her we were painting the roof. In total amazement, she said, "The gold??" One of the other guys was moving to tell her about the roof when I jumped in with, "Yeah, why do you think we are so shiny?"

"But the paint on you is green."

"It's the way the sunlight shines on it. Go out, look, and see where we have painted."

The following day we were back in the snack shop.

"Hey, I went outside and looked. I didn't see anything."

"Which side of the building were you on?"

"The east side"

"Oh, we are working on the west side. Try again."

Next Day.

"I looked and still didn't see it."

"It must have already dried. Once it dries, you can't tell the difference. Look at the north side this afternoon."

Bad Dan. Bad, bad Dan.

THE FSRA

The following is a transcript of a recent press conference held by John Smith, the Under Secretary of the FSRB:

Hello, my name is John Smith. I am currently the Under Secretary of the recently created FSRB...the Federal Syllable Reduction Bureau. The FSRB was created in accordance with the FSRA, or the Federal Syllable Reduction Act of 2021. The FSRA was enacted to ensure that the Average American has access to, and an understanding of, everyday conversation.

As a bit of history, the FSRA was proposed when two senators were having lunch one day. They noticed it took the waiter approximately three minutes to tell them that the special was baked chicken... basted in something. They both looked at each other and said, "There ought to be a law." And thus, the FSRA came to be.

The point of the FSRA is, "Why waste all those words and energy?" At a minimum, the overuse of words wastes everyone's time, making many of the population feel awkward and inadequate. The two sponsoring senators were able to add a one-million-dollar rider to a military weapons bill to fund a study. The study's premise was this, "Certainly, polysyllabic people know they are polysyllabic but do monosyllabic people know they are monosyllabic?"

The study was able to conclude the vocabulary of the "Average American" and that of those above average and those below average. When study groups were asked the premise question, those who ranked above average generally responded, "Certainly, everyone would know if they are polysyllabic." Those in the study group that fell below average replied that they had been listening in stereo for years.

Average is, of course, the operative word here. The overhead graph you now see behind me (Please see the attached chart) shows that the people above this line (point A on your chart) are entirely conversant with complex word scenarios and would welcome the mental stimulation of a one-hundred-fifty-word description of "baked chicken." Everyone below this line (point B on your chart) simply asked, "Is it fried?"

To borrow a phrase from our EPA friends, the main thrust of the FSRA is to condition Americans to reduce their "syllable footprint." Thereby being less verbose in conversation. According to the study, one of the best ways to accomplish this is to never use the word "verbose." Additional sections of the FSRA provide penalties for using words that are overly... well... long. Using a fifty-cent word when a ten-cent word is perfectly appropriate is now illegal.

I have made changes in my life to reflect my support of the spirit of the FSRA and my dedication to the charter of the FSRB. As many of you may have guessed by my appearance and accent, I am a Hispanic American. My birth name is Juan Ramirez Hidalgo Rodriguez Montevalla Valdez. I changed my name to John Smith so people would have less to remember. Of course, my mother now hates me.

It is the greatest desire of the FSRB that you of the press corps embrace this new era in American communication. You will be at the forefront of this realignment of the American people to this new way of life.

Understanding that every new law of this type has unforeseen problems with implementation, the FSRB has designed a process by which certain people or groups may be exempt from the requirements of the FSRA. For example, publishers of dictionaries will be able to maintain a catalog of words that would otherwise be prohibited under the FSRA, providing any published version contains a warning about content. Applications for other exemptions are being accepted at the FSRB offices here in DC.

Under the current structure of the FSRA, no exemptions will be granted for cable news announcers or pundits. Violators will be fined based on the number of letters in the sentence in which the offending word, or words, is used. Which reminds me. You may now complete a sentence with a preposition.

Remember the FSRB motto: An extensive vocabulary is best used for listening.

Thank you. I can take your questions now.

GIZMOS*

Cars being what they are to our lives, we have come to expect a substantial amount of creature comforts from them and a healthy portion of gizmos. Gizmos are traditionally viewed as guy things, but over the last few decades, it has become evident that both sexes like their toys. No, wait... uh. Both sexes like their... well, let's stick to gizmos.

Modern SUVs are highly advanced when compared to the original mini-vans. Talk about gizmos. Wow!! Electric sliding doors. Twin stereos. They even have a proximity sensor that beeps at you when you get close to an object (or person) while backing up. Buck Rogers, eat your heart out. Come to think of it... Buck Rogers probably wouldn't be jealous until the proximity sensor vaporizes whatever it is (object or person) that you are about to back into. Hey, can't be late for tennis.

I like my gizmos like anybody else. Though cruise control has been around for a long time, it is undoubtedly my all-time favorite. I still remember the first time I set the cruise on a car, and the gas pedal pulled away from my foot. What a weird feeling. Almost like that falling feeling you get just before you go to sleep. You know you are there; you just don't feel in control. My other favorite is the automatic electric window. One touch. Down they go. One touch. Up they go. The drive-through is so much easier. Look, Ma, no hands!

Of all the gizmos I have, I wonder why my car has a tachometer. Am I going to "red line" a modern sedan? The car has 350 computers built in. Get one of them to take care of that. Tachometers are a throwback from when gears didn't change automatically, and men liked to talk RPMs instead of IPOs. When I was a teenager, a guy I knew said he used his tach to figure out his speed instead of the speedometer since it was more accurate. This means, of course, that he would have to know the ratio of every gear in the transmission and differential as well as the circumference of the rear tires AND be able to mentally perform complex mathematical calculations without dropping the ashes off the end of his cigarette. I was in class with this guy. I don't think so.

Years and years ago - exact date withheld to protect my ego - I had a 1969 Pontiac GTO that had a tachometer, even though it had an automatic transmission. It was a bit "souped up" looking but tame enough. I didn't hesitate to let my mother use it when she needed to borrow a car for a few weeks. The day I got the car back from her, we were all sitting around talking and drinking coffee. Mom told me she thought something was wrong with the speedometer on the car, and I then asked why. She said that even at a complete stop, the speedometer was jumping between 7 and 9 miles per hour. I choked, and coffee flew out of my mouth and nose. Some of you already know what happened. After I caught my breath, I knew I had turned gray with the realization that she had been using the tachometer as the speedometer. I didn't know the gear ratios. I didn't know the circumference of my rear tires. I did know that if the tach said "30" (= 3000 RPM), the speedometer was usually around 60 MPH.

"Mother, didn't you notice the other big dial that pointed to "0" when you were sitting still?"

"No."

"Uhhh... when you thought you were driving 35 MPH, you were probably going about 70!"

"Ohhhh... maybe that's why your sister was hanging onto the door handle so tight."

And this is the woman that wouldn't let me run with scissors in my hand.

A 9 OR A 2*

You'd never know you were a 9 unless there were some 2's running around.

All of our lives, we are exposed to comparisons and the importance of measuring one's - or another's - accomplishments in life. When we are born, the nurses measure and weigh us right after a good slap to ensure we pay attention. Then the proclamation, "This one is a keeper." or "Maybe we should have left this one in for a little longer." And Mom and Dad don't just send pictures; they put the statistics right on that card. Coochie Coo. Of course, if they didn't, Aunt Hilda would ask anyway because Bobby - her darling little snookums - took 42 and a half hours of labor, was 23 inches, 10 pounds 8 ounces, came out feet first, had a full head of hair, and had a date with Nurse Johnson before he hit the incubator. Two years later, all the little bastard can do is piss on your couch. "Isn't he a darling!"

Twins, especially, must have a deep-seated competition problem. "I was born first, and I'm the oldest." "I was an inch longer, and I'm the biggest." "I weighed four more ounces; you were an underachiever." "No, I wasn't; you pinched my umbilical." "I have the top bunk; I can oversee my domain." "I have the bottom bunk; I can go to the bathroom without waking up." "I have the top bunk 'cause you're too stupid to climb the ladder." "You have the top bunk 'cause it doesn't matter if you fall and hit your head."

Then, our educational process rates and grades us like a #2 tomato. (Admittedly, I don't know what a #2 tomato is) First, there is the alphabet. A, B, C, D, you know the rest. You do, don't you? And to fully exemplify the importance of the alphabet, we got our classroom seats by alphabetical placement. Zeus may have been the God of Gods, but he would have been in the last chair on the right in Miss Harris' classroom. And NO passing notes to Athena. After getting a good handle on the alphabet as a de-motivator, we have our first test. Graded on - you got it - the alphabet.

Since I was a "B" and a damn good one, I had pretty good access to the front of the room and, therefore, learning. Think about it. All through history, it plays the same. Aristotle sat up front. So did Beethoven, Bach, and Chopin. And Einstein was on the right side but definitely "front row."

I know what you are thinking, "How did Socrates get so smart?" Simple, really - the Greeks had fewer letters than we do. I don't even think they had an "S," so he probably said his name was Alan. Test it for yourself. Next time you meet someone named Watkins, see if they don't stretch their neck while you are talking to see if they can hear you better.

Of course, it goes on and on through our formative years. We don't go to the "next" grade; we go to a "higher" grade - unless your name was Watkins. You go from Elementary to Middle school and then to High school. In English, we are taught superlatives like "good, better, best" or "dumb, dumber, dumbest." We have older brothers and older sisters. All we get to do is kick the dog. The class yearbook always honors the students recognized as superior by calling them the "Most Congenial," the "Most Intelligent," and the "Most Likely to Succeed." Get this, though. Since these people didn't give themselves this honor, they were voted there by the people that were "Least Congenial," "Least Intelligent," and "Least Likely to Succeed." How could they have been right? They have no personality, no idea why they are in the back row, and will probably get a job as a Driver's License Examiner so they can cheat on their eye test. But you, Mr. Congenial, have gained their respect.

Competition is the hallmark of the American adult. If you aren't competitive, then please stand to the side. Jobs and possessions are where this shows up the most. No sooner than we clear our attempt at higher education and wipe the sweat from our brows, there is another ladder to climb. We get a job that we hope will be a career, and the scramble for us to stay ahead of our contemporaries begins. We wear the right shoes, drive the right car, and have the right golf clubs just to find out that the father of the Watkins kid owns the company.

Home is where the race continues, only in khaki pants. "So, Bob. How many square feet did you add to your house? I have been thinking about remodeling a little myself." "So, Bob, does that mower have a 10-horsepower engine or a 14, like mine?" "So, Bob, just how big are Mary's boobs since the implants?" Men are generally more competitive than women, but even if women aren't competitive in their careers, they can join in their husbands' attempts at stardom. "My husband gave me an emerald ring for Valentine's Day." "My husband gave me a diamond ring for Valentine's Day." "My husband gave me - and his mistress - a diamond ring for Valentine's Day." Top that one, Bitch.

Any way you look at it, people are constantly comparing themselves to others and others to themselves. The question remains. What is the measure of a man? I have compiled a list of how different people generally - measure a man. I have used only the most reliable data, arrived at by the best research.

A: measures a man:

Greedy man - by the size of the wallet

Philanthropist - by the generosity of his wallet

Preacher - by the generosity of his soul

Crook - by how big a bank you have robbed

Stockbroker - how big was that bank? And what are your plans for your windfall?

Salesman - by what it takes to "earn" your business

Garbageman - by how neat the plastic bag is tied

Pharmacist - by Name brand or "Generic"

Tailor - with a tape measure

Computer Geek - by how much RAM you have

Woman - by his sentiment and thoughtfulness

Gold-digger - see Greedy Man

Nymphomaniac - see Tailor

HAIR LOSS*

While at the optometrist's shop, I was killing time sitting in the fitting area, waiting for the clerk to bring me some contacts. They have mirrors everywhere so people can see their appearance in their glasses. As I scanned the walls, I nearly jumped out of my chair when I got to one of the angled mirrors. The multi-mirror reflection gave me an excellent view of a big bald spot on the back of my head. AAAGGGHHHHH!!!!

You know... you get so used to seeing yourself from one particular angle that it is shocking to see yourself this way. I think I must usually close my eyes when the stylist puts the hand mirror up to show me the back of my head after a haircut. It isn't as if my hair loss was news to me. My hairline had been receding for fifteen years, and I was used to seeing my hair from the front... or should I say, I am used to <u>not</u> seeing my hair from the front. But this... this makes me look like one of those monks. You know... it starts with a "B"... "B something," something Monks. No... maybe it begins with an "F." Oh well, you know what I am saying.

I should be happy. My expanding follicle desert has been an unending source of fun for my daughter. "Dad... can you turn a little to the left... more... yeah, that's it. Thanks, the sun was shining off your forehead."

Ha. Ha. Funny.

My dad died when he was sixty-two, and his hair was thin and patterned just about the way mine is now. I guess I should feel better knowing that I will stay pretty much this way... that is if his condition is an indication for me. I shouldn't be too worried, though. People have always said I look a bit like a couple of famous actors with expansive foreheads. Especially when I am wearing shades. They seem to do well. Hmmm... I guess that could be the money, though. Maybe fame. Talent... stuff like that. "Do 'well' at what?" you ask. Why women, of course. What else would a single guy be thinking about? Well... money, I suppose... of course, so he can afford to attract women. And then more money... so he can afford to divorce them.

Women always pay attention to hair, and we know it. Samson... he had hair, he had strength. Delilah wanted him. Cut his hair off. No strength. No Delilah. You never saw a classic leading man that was bald without his toupee until he was old enough to play the part of an old bald guy. Many women say, "Oh, I like hair like that. Why would you even think about it? You look good." And then comes the inevitable follower, "Your hair is just like my dad's!" I think most guys will agree that when they are meeting/dating a woman, they don't want to be told they remind her of her "daddy." It takes the whole thing and... well... just weird.

Unless you're into that kind of thing.

This is not an issue that I am going to do something overwhelmingly stupid over. I am not going out and getting a hairpiece, weave, or anything like that. Fake is so obvious. There aren't too many men in their forties with "bangs" with that poofy spot with a part in the middle. You know the look. Get real. Or a comb-over. Woohoo... that's a GQ look. I saw a guy the other day that looked like he had a "comb-up"... up from the hair on his back!!

Transplant, though... now we're talking.

VIVA LA RESOLUCIONNE'

New Year's 2002

Another New Year is here, and we must face the inevitable challenge to all humans - the New Year's Resolutions. Personally, I try to avoid the words "New Year's Resolution." I think that any attempt at self-improvement that comes the day after a party where you eat twenty-two boiled shrimp, a half pound of prime rib, four dinner rolls, three pastry-looking things that you have no idea what they were stuffed with, God knows what else and washed it all down with fifteen bourbon and colas. Well, that attempt may be couched in failure. That is why I wait until about a week into the new year to make any worthless promises to myself if I do it at all.

Did you see yourself in the mirror on New Year's morning? Could that face be the one saying, "This is the first day of the rest of your life! What are you going to do with it?"

Your probable answer: "Well... first... I am... going to... throw... up."

I do make some plans that others may think of as resolutions. I want to drink less, not smoke, and go to the gym more. I do well with smoking since I never have smoked, but I get a well-deserved pat on the back for my effort. That leaves drinking and exercise. I figured, "Drinking is easy, just don't have any."(haha!)

Going to the gym is more like it. I never have exercised enough, but I do enjoy it. And I didn't just start either, so when I went to the gym on January the 2nd, I thought of how I felt right at home when I walked in. Wait a minute. I didn't know that feeling at home meant it would be like eighteen people living in a one-room shack like you see on those TV commercials when people ask for your money.

The gym was crowded with people. It was so crowded that all the stationary bikes had two people each - one on the left pedal and one on the right. A whistle would blow every two minutes so they could all run to the other side. My eyes rolled back into my head as I realized... the gym had been taken over by Resolutionaries. You know, the ones. All wearing the same uniforms... spandex they got for Christmas. I once wrote the FTC and asked if they could put a warning tag on all spandex products. They said they were more concerned about flammability tags than ones that said, "Warning: This material may make you look like an idiot."

Seeing the futility of trying for any of the bikes or treadmills, I went into the weight room. It wasn't any better. You had to sign a waiting list for each machine. I get to do bicep curls a week from next Wednesday.

I heard one guy yelling, "You can do it! Go for it! Pull!" I thought he was giving a pep talk to a fellow weight-lifter until I saw he was trying to help his wife snug up her spandex. By the way, when you buy spandex....one size does NOT fit all.

I had all I could take and left. I was so disappointed that I went to a bar for drinks. I wrote all this down on bar napkins while taking in the secondhand smoke from the guy beside me. Oh well. I resigned myself to the fact that it was too difficult to do anything at the same time as everyone else.

As soon as I finish this, I will start my Valentine's Day resolutions list.

NEW YEAR'S 2006

Well... here we are again. Another New Year's Day is behind us, and the new year is ahead. I am opposed to resolutions, as they tend to make me all too aware of how bad I am at keeping them. So, I continue my custom of declaring that the only resolution I wish to make is to make no resolution. Something I am quite resolute about.

Now, even though I do not make resolutions, I can't help but feel a little different with the arrival of the New Year. We all feel we should do something to renew ourselves and dust off our life. Move some furniture. Hang a new picture. Clean out the refrigerator.

I don't know about the rest of you, but I tend to let things sit around too long despite my generally high level of attention to detail. You know. You see something on the floor or the table that you could quickly put away but allow it to stay till Saturday. After a couple of days, it becomes part of the décor - so to speak - and it begins to get less visual attention than it should. And it isn't just because I am a single guy living alone. You girls do the same thing, so wipe that knowing smirk off your face!

I shouldn't tell on myself, but I can't help but pass it on. The other day I noticed that the top shelf of my refrigerator seemed a tad on the "high-density" side. I am tall, so when I open the refrigerator door, I look down and only see the front of the top shelf. It is a geometric thing, like the horizon. You can't see England because of the earth's curvature, and I can't see the back of the top shelf because I am tall.

Well, since I had that "renewal" thing running through my veins today, I took a closer look at what was on that shelf. In a labor-saving effort, I pulled the garbage can closer. There was a milk carton lurking. It was a bit of a surprise. I only buy milk when I get cereal, and I was trying to remember when the last time was. When was that, anyway? Well, ok. Here's the bottom line. The expiration date was last February. Egad!!

Several years ago, I did declare at my business that our resolution was to "scrape the barnacles!" As a ship sits in the water, it collects barnacles on the hull. Those barnacles must be scraped from the hull so the ship can move through the water faster and with less effort. Like a ship, we must "scrape those barnacles" from our lives. Get rid of those things that have attached themselves to us, the things that slow us down, the things that burden us every day, the things that stand in our way, and the things at the back of the top shelf!

So, here is my New Year's challenge to you. Whether you "scrape the barnacles" or go on a diet or start yoga classes... do it for other reasons than because it is a new year. Do it because you woke up this morning and decided to make it part of your day.

If you wake up tomorrow and decide to, you can do it again. Then, if you wake up one morning and decide not to do it again, you are off the hook without guilt. Unless, of course, you talk to your mother that day.

Somebody, please tell me if you have had an expiration date older than mine?

Happy New Year!

POLITICS AND RELIGION

Not a Chance

THE GRAND CONSPIRACY*

Reviewing the big event, I was talking to a woman friend on Thanksgiving Day. After the usual turkey talk, the conversation got to shopping on Black Friday. I don't usually try to get out since it is so crowded. It is a day for professionals. I don't think I have shopped on the "biggest shopping day of the year" in over twenty years, but I had already decided to brave it and go to the mall this year. My friend explained that she and her mother would go shopping together... something they do every year. "Well... that's nice that y'all get together like that."

So, on Friday, I went to the mall. I like to people-watch, so the larger crowd would make the stroll from store to store much more interesting. I had been in the mall for about a half hour and thought of what my friend had said. She and her mother went together... not she and her family... just she and her mother. As I looked around the corridors, I saw a few guys, a few guys and girls, and a few girls by themselves. Overwhelmingly though, everywhere I looked, there were mothers and daughters. There were even grandmothers, daughters, and granddaughters.

I thought, "What a cool thing that all these daughters are here with their moms. Walking, talking, enjoying the fellowship of shopping together."

Hey. Wait a minute. Suddenly, a cold feeling hit me as the hair stood up on the back of my neck. This is where they get it. The "training." I stopped in my tracks. If this had been a movie, there would have been a camera dizzily swirling around me.

The shopping thing isn't instinct, after all. It is a trained response... And there I was in the middle of the training ground. I looked to the left and the right. Yes, that's it. They were everywhere. And in teams. Some moms were 40 years old with 20-year-old daughters, and 40-year-old daughters were with 60-year-old moms. They come back every year for refresher courses in basic over-shopping. I began to worry that they could look at my face and sense that I had figured it out. As the stark reality of the moment grew in my mind, I kept expecting a black hood was about to be thrown over my head as I was pushed into a van.

This explains a lot of things. About the first of November, you know how your wife gets. "Honey, don't make any plans for the day after Thanksgiving. You know I want you to go shopping with Mom and me." And a week later, "I know things are busy at work but don't even think about going to the office the day after Thanksgiving. We are going shopping and plan to stay most of the day." And then, the Monday before Thanksgiving, "Sweetie, we think we can make it to two malls and an outlet center if we have your help." What fresh hell is this? All the while you think they want you there and whenever shopping is mentioned you wonder what you could do to get out of it. Think, man, think.

But, all became clear to me that day. This is just a clever ploy to get you to go to the office or, their favorite, get you to go golfing or hunting or something for the entire weekend.

Yes. I have discovered the secret. My life may be in danger for revealing it. I don't know what can be done. Probably nothing at this point... the social imprinting has been going on for centuries. The most we can gain from this is the knowledge itself, and perhaps... with this awareness... we can one day learn to go shopping with them, at least in self-defense from the conspiracy that besets us.

NAH!! Let's go golfing or hunting or something.

THE LOTION BOTTLE

What makes us think we should decorate, coordinate, arrange, match, complement, and organize anyway?

The question is this. Which came first... the need to spruce up your kitchen and bath or the bed and bath superstores? Did we need a store to provide us with cute, trendy accessories, or did the mere existence of the store spark a desire to have all that stuff?

I had a perfectly good toothbrush holder - the bathroom counter. All you have to do is lay the brush down on the counter, and it will be there when you get back. Granted, you should lay the toothbrush down with the bristles pointing up. It is the germ-fighting thing to do. After all, if the bristles touch the counter, some nasty germs that grow in your mouth may find their way onto the counter. And then what would happen?

So, I was in this bed and bath store buying new cookware, previously called frying pans. Across the aisle was the bathroom accessory section. I meandered. They had at least fifty different styles of sets of toothbrush holders/soap dishes/lotion dispensers. Some with matching trash bins. For the exercise, I walked up and down the aisle several times, looking at the various sets when one caught my eye. I said to myself, "Now that would go well in my bath!" There are medications for such thoughts. I am not currently on any, so I bought this bathroom accessory set.

To my surprise, the set looked very lovely in my bathroom. Its color, clean lines, and shape all came together harmoniously. In full disclosure, I heard that one day as I was channel surfing.

The toothbrush holder is a four-holer. More than enough for one toothbrush. Then I thought, "Why four holes?" Is this a leftover from the olden days when an entire family used one bathroom? Am I supposed to have more than one toothbrush? Regardless, the counter is now safe from my germs.

The soap dish is simple enough. You lay soap in it, and every couple of months, you use the leftover soap to wash it clean. The lotion pump was next. I keep a bottle of lotion on the counter to get "instant relief" from the dry skin around my elbows. The lotion comes in an entirely adequate plastic bottle, but I decided to set up the dispenser since it was part of the set. Again, simple enough. Just pour the lotion from the bottle into the new dispenser. I have successfully poured things from bottle to bottle plenty of times in the past. I quickly found out that lotion does not "pour." The bottle and the dispenser had openings about a half inch in diameter. At least with most liquids, the pouring source stream would reduce in size during the pouring process and fit right into the receiving bottle.

Any lotion that came out of the bottle was in a half-inch diameter... glop. When first attempting the transfer, what happened was that the glop sat on top of the dispenser opening and wouldn't ooze right in because the half-inch glop made an airtight seal which kept the half-inch glop from dropping into the dispenser. Hmmm. A solution must be found. The solution had to be found quickly because the half-inch diameter glop was also above the rim of the dispenser opening. Since it would not run into the dispenser, it began to run down the side.

It occurred to me that if I broke the seal created by the half-inch glop, it would probably allow the lotion to flow smoothly into the dispenser. Success. The lotion would now go into the dispenser.

Now that I had gotten past that problem, I needed more lotion at the mouth of the bottle. What did I do? I shook the bottle down... without covering the opening. A glop... one-half inch in diameter and approximately three inches long now sat on my counter. Oops. Well, I didn't want to throw it away, so I grabbed it - as much as you can grab lotion - and began feeding it into the dispenser's opening. Between the original glop oozing down the side of the dispenser and my trying to force-feed the new glop, the dispenser and the surrounding area were getting a bit slippery. I was beginning to laugh out loud.

And now, for my next number.

The lotion was finally going into the dispenser, so I decided to speed up the process by squeezing the bottle. Oops, Part II.

I don't know how big that glop was. However, I know it was a half-inch in diameter and long enough to coat the entire bathroom counter. By now, I am laughing my ass off and thinking I am trapped in some TV episode where everything that can go wrong does.

So, there I was, with lotion on my arms, hands, and most everything within a couple of feet of me, laughing uncontrollably, just glad no one could see... and, all the while, wishing someone was there just to laugh with me. Or at me, I am ok with that!

Had someone walked in, I am sure I would have had some "splaining to do."

THE VERGE OF SANITY

Many of my friends know that I generally take the month of June off from drinking. What many of them don't know is that toward the end of one June... I sought my doctor's help for one of the unpleasant side effects of my sabbatical:

Doc: So... what's the problem?

Dan: Well... it is hard to explain, but I have been seeing things.

Doc: Things? Do you mean like seeing snakes on the wall?

Dan: No

Doc: How about pink elephants?

Dan: No

Doc: A fiscal Liberal with a sound argument?

Dan: Doc... get serious... at least the first two exist!

Doc: Go on, then.

Dan: I get up in the morning and can see more clearly than I remember. And it happens as soon as I open my eyes. It used to take an hour to not see double in the mornings.

Doc: Anything else?

Dan: I smell things - the coffee, the bacon... and I think clearly... that's been happening too!

Doc: Hmmm... do go on

Dan: I don't know... SO many things are clear now. I used to walk down the hall and forget why I was walking. Now I always remember everything.

Doc: I see... have you been calmer than usual?... are you more focused?

Dan: Yes. Doc, why are you taking notes? Why... why are you shaking your head? Tell me, Doc... be straight with me!

Doc: Dan... you may want to sit down.

Dan: I am sitting

Doc: Oh... then I will... This is just an educated guess, and we will need to do more tests, but I think you may have adult onset of CCC, Cerebral Cogno Claritus.

Dan: Doc... cut the Latin double talk. I can take it...

Doc: I think you may be on the verge of... sanity...

Dan: Sanity??? No... that can't be. I am still so young. I still have so much of my life to screw up.

Doc: Please... be calm... the other patients may hear.

Dan: I don't understand. I've never been exposed. There's no family history... maybe that one uncle... but we always wondered if he was adopted. What do I do? Will my lifestyle change?

Doc: It won't be so bad... research is making continual strides with conditions like these, and new drugs are constantly being developed. In the meantime, it may help to paint your walls with "no-gloss" eggshell white, eat only iceberg lettuce in your salads, no pepper, and only local & network tv - no cable. This brochure, Coping with Mental Sharpness, has a complete list of recommendations.

Dan: What will all that do?

Doc: We find that by filling your life with the most boring surroundings possible, then, by contrast, sanity may seem a little more... well... acceptable. Less of a shock to the system. The sooner, the better. CCC is a progressive degenerative disease, and I can't tell you how much longer you may be able to have an abnormal life.

Dan: But... can't you take a guess?

Doc: Perhaps. Tell me... have you taken out an IRA?

Dan: No, but I bought some blue chip stocks the other day.

Doc: You had better start painting now.

THERAPY*

When someone starts to see a therapist, a specific event usually triggers the need to go to counseling. Marital problems. Divorce. The loss of a job.

I went to a therapist after the loss of a job. After a couple of sessions, he asked if I was thinking about returning to work at the same thing or if I was considering a career change. I told him I was thinking about becoming a stand-up comedian. I was encouraged when he broke out in laughter.

It seemed late in my life to become a stand-up comic. I have always had the requisite mental dysfunction but didn't have time to work on my material. Now that I had been in therapy, I figured I could do stand-up. All stand-up comics do bits about their time in therapy. I could see myself on stage saying:

> "Has anyone else been through counseling? Come on. Fess up. Ok - two things just happened. Some of you didn't raise your hand because you don't want your date to know - so you haven't really dealt with your fear of rejection yet. The ones who raised your hand just let your date know they need to sleep with a gun under their pillow."

I know - find another day job.

For whatever reason, you start going to a therapist. There is a point at which you open up to the idea and begin to self-examine. Once you start going to those hidden places in your mind, you begin finding your internal monsters. You think the stuff in your refrigerator for a few months is scary. Try going into the deep recesses of your mind to find things that have been there for thirty or forty years. You know... you end up dragging stuff out of your subconscious that would make those guys from slasher movies go to confession... "forgive me, Father, for I have sinned. I killed thirty-two people last night... and... I... just... can't... find... love."

It is essential to find the right therapist, though. I went to one guy, and as I left after the first session, he asked if I was feeling suicidal. When I said, "No, I don't. Why do you ask?" he said, "Well, after listening to you for an hour - I do."

I went back to the same guy the following week. He said that I was repressing my hostilities, and then he told me I needed to find a way to vent my anger and frustrations... so I shot him.

So... when you move to a new state, you start looking for a new therapist.

One of the most awkward things about going to therapy is getting to the office, walking into the waiting room, and finding someone else already there. First, you are a little self-conscious about anyone else knowing you are there. Then, if you did say anything to them, what would it be, "How are you?" They would probably say, "Fine," but it's a therapist's office. How could they be "Fine?" Then you start to think, I know what I'm here for. I wonder what's wrong with them. I know I'm ok, but are they ok? What if they think they are ok and wonder if I'm ok. What if they aren't ok but don't know they aren't ok, and they think I'm not ok. What if they are so not ok that they think I'm so not ok that I could hurt them. Then, just because they are so not ok that they think I am so un-ok that I may harm them, they may just do something to hurt me before I can hurt them. But I am ok enough to understand what they are thinking, so I start thinking about what to do if they do something first. Then I think that if I wait till they do something first, they might catch me off-guard and hurt me. Maybe I should go ahead and break this lamp over their head.

Setting all that aside. Therapy has helped me to become a new-age man of the 90s - sensitive, understanding, and open. Unfortunately, the 90s are over, and in the new millennium, it will be hip to be distrusting and aggressive and not give a damn what your mother thinks about anything.

Can I get a refund?

SECTION IV: MISCELLANY AND THOUGHTS

You should know yourself well enough to be aware of your weaknesses and appreciative of your strengths. Besides a strong thirst for knowledge, my strengths focus on the observation of life around me. In particular, behavior patterns of others and myself.

These are stories that don't really fit into the Humor or Relationship category, though they may be partially about relationships, and you may find parts humorous. But they weren't written specifically to be about relationships, but some facet of life, funny or not.

SIMPLIFIED

For those who don't already know, "McMansion" is a term for a beautiful, large house in a subdivision full of beautiful, large houses. The kind of house that would have once qualified as a mansion, except that it is built and "stamped out" in a somewhat cookie-cutter fashion.

In the pre-rideshare era, I had the pleasure of being the designated driver for four women as we all went to a friend's birthday party. I say pleasure. Being a designated driver is a pleasure while driving to a party, and it isn't so bad at the party. However, being the only person yet to have several glasses of wine and a couple of tequila shots makes the drive home slightly different from the drive there. As I drove home, I was informed of every all-night diner that I passed on the way. My riders expressed a bit of consternation that I was not the least bit interested in stopping. I was focused on getting back to the house so I could have a shot of tequila. (then we would go eat)

At The Party

As I mentioned, the birthday girl lives in a lovely house, and as we looked around, we went into the dining room, where the food was set up. One of the women, Betty, pointed and said, "Look, malted milk balls!"

Her voice and expression showed a touch of surprise with

a healthy portion of fascination. She picked a couple up and handed one to me and two more of our friends.

As I was eating mine, one of the others said, "It's Easter!" I automatically remembered that I got malted milk balls in my Easter baskets when I was a kid. I don't think I have seen a malted milk ball since I got Easter baskets, but as soon as we all saw them, we all had a response that was most likely based on long-forgotten yet still cherished childhood memories.

Betty commented that she had been to many excellent parties where pâté and caviar were served but never expected to see malted milk balls at a party in a McMansion! It was an antithetical culinary experience. The look of fascination did not leave her face as she enjoyed this simple pleasure. It was as if Betty had, for a moment, left behind the things that burdened her, the things in her life that didn't turn out the way she had planned, the things she had to do "tomorrow."

Simple pleasure. I pondered the moment and thought of how I had heard someone speak or, perhaps, I read somewhere that occasionally, you should skip rather than walk as it was virtually impossible to not smile as you skip.

Life as a grown-up can get complicated. Jobs, children, family, exes, houses, cars, shopping, cooking, cleaning, exercising, carpooling, and the nuances of interpersonal relations accompanying all of life's moments can take their toll. Taking time out for a pleasurable moment can be difficult. When it does come, it is often as complicated as everything else we do. There is just no skipping anymore.

In our broadband, cellular phone, and satellite dish lives, what we really crave is simplicity. A few moments, however long, when we are disconnected. A time when you can get 3 blocks from your house, realize you left your cell phone, and not turn around. A toasted cheese sandwich instead of a panini. Kool-Aid instead of trendy flavored vitamin water.

"Simplified" has been part of the tagline for my business for several years. Another marketing friend once noted that the good thing about "Simplified" is that it can mean different things to different people. It depends on what a person may need or feel when seeing it. One person may think it means cheaper. Another may think quicker, and still, another may think easier.

Apparently... for some... simplified means eating malted milk balls at a party in a McMansion.

BIRTHDAYS*

An acquaintance once asked me what I was doing for the July 4th weekend. I told her that the 4th was my birthday and that I hadn't made my final plans yet. She and a couple of other people there commented on how nice it must be to have July 4th as my birthday, and they hoped I had a good birthday. I have learned to appreciate that almost everyone, myself included, likes to get some attention on their birthday. After all, all other holidays are about events, remembrances, or the like, but your birthday is your day of celebration. Not because you are a father, mother, veteran, or anything else, but just because you are you.

Many years ago, I took up the practice of trying to find out the birthday of people I meet. I keep birthday reminders in my calendar and write, call, or e-mail the person close to the special day. I do this whenever I meet someone I expect to maintain contact with over a longer term.

Some time ago, I gave a birthday call to one of the employees in a new division of our company. I called Bob about thirty minutes after he arrived at work and simply said, "Hi, Bob. Happy Birthday!" There was a moment of silence, and then he responded, with sincere appreciation, "Man... thanks for that. My wife didn't even say Happy Birthday to me this morning." He then went on with several more words of appreciation for my taking the time to call him. After that, he talked about work, how well things were going, and how he enjoyed the company. I was almost overwhelmed by the level of response that the call had created. And I was pretty happy that the moment I had taken out of my day had made such an apparent difference in his day. I am no longer with the company, and when I left, I could not get my birthday database off the computer. I sure hope Bob's wife remembers this year.

I haven't always been so engaged when it comes to birthdays. I mentioned earlier that I have learned to appreciate the fact that most people enjoy getting attention on their birthday. I remember having parties when I was much younger - very few candles. I still have some of the pictures from back then. Somewhere over time, the event became less important to me. From eighteen to thirty-five, I worked in retail and another job where you definitely have to work on the 4th of July. In reflection, I think that as my birthday became "less special," so did everyone else's.

My first shock back to reality was when I was engaged to my second wife - and forgot her birthday. Bad move. Her family had always made great ado over birthdays, and she did not understand how I could have been so insensitive. Now, as I look back, I know she was right. I managed to flower, card, and poem my way back into her graces and didn't forget that day again for the nine years we were together. And, for her thirtieth birthday, I even threw a big surprise party. I had about twenty of our friends and family waiting on her at the restaurant. That finally got me out of the "time when I forgot..." annual recollection. I even sent her a card six years after the divorce.

What really made me focus on birthdays' was my 40th.

It was my first birthday after the divorce, and I know I felt a bit lonely then. I had a really nice group of friends, and one of them had a party at his house for the 4th. My friends went out of their way to make the event a party for me, separate from the other festivities. I don't think I had felt so childlike about a birthday in thirty years. It was that day (well, probably the next day after the hangover wore off) that I decided to make more of an effort to treat others to some attention on their birthday. Since then, I have surprised many people with a call or a note on their birthday. I knew they would feel good from the recognition, but I have found that I get as much enjoyment out of it as they do. Too bad I didn't start earlier.

MIDDLE AGE SANE

Though some may disagree, one of the many things I have learned in middle age is to speak less in absolutes. I have learned that it is better to represent myself as having experienced or observed things, and thereby I have come to my own conclusions as to what they mean. Some of those conclusions may have a degree of meaning to others, so I write them down and pass them on… like leaving breadcrumbs for those that end up on the same path as, or at least one similar to, mine.

Middle Aged Crazy is something I have heard of all my life. I have listened to stories and songs and seen movies portraying someone as "middle age crazy" or, to save my fingers from so much typing, MAC. In these stories, it is almost always a man who goes MAC, and he invariably buys a sports car and chases younger women. In and of themselves, those two things don't really reek of "crazy," but they definitely stink of "expensive." Both cost a lot to obtain, and once you have them, they are often in the shop for makeovers and repairs. You usually spend more time talking about them than actually showing them off.

But the point here is more about my thoughts that MAC isn't about being crazy at all. It is about being free. We spend our entire childhood becoming adolescents, and we spend our adolescence becoming adults. Then we spend our adulthood becoming our own parents. When do we get to just "be" instead of always "becoming?" I propose that, usually, Middle Age Crazy is the point at which we understand that we are in charge of our own lives and can do anything we want. Anything.

An oft-used anecdote about self-limitation is that of the elephant and his tether, so I will use the example again. As the story goes, a baby elephant is chained by his leg to a post that he can not break away from, no matter how hard he tries. Each day the elephant is chained to the post. Each day the elephant pulls against the chain to no avail, until one day, he gives up and never pulls again. From then on, the giant will remain in the same place until the next day when the chain is removed. Once this training is complete, all the owner needs to do is tie a rope from a stake in the ground to the elephant's leg, and the elephant will stay in place. This, the elephant does, though being fully capable of breaking the rope with one decisive move on his part. The elephant is free and doesn't even know it.

We act much the same way. We are trained from childhood to "become" something... a "something" that someone else has described to us and that most of us just accept as our life's work. With our heads down and noses to the grindstone, we get out of school, get a job, get married, and have kids... putting little check marks next to each line on the list that is our life. For about twenty years, most of us never look up. We are invisibly and inextricably tethered to the list.

I don't know if elephants are actually afraid of mice. But if they are, what does a tethered elephant do when a mouse runs in front of it? If, out of his complacency, he is startled and moves a few feet to the side, he will doubtlessly snap the tether before realizing what he is doing. For whatever reason, some of us come to a point in our life where we are startled... perhaps presented with a situation profoundly out of our normal scope. As reasoning creatures, we recognize that we have just done something we didn't think we could or even had "permission" to try. Once the boundary has moved, we begin to test other unknowns and soon find ourselves thinking and acting quite differently.

Imagine having the same checking account for twenty years. You work along, getting by, never really doing anything extraordinary or unusual. Then one day, you balance the checkbook and discover that you have had a million dollars for the last ten years and just didn't realize it. An unlikely scenario, but do you think you will act crazy, or do you think you will just act "free"?

Others will likely see your newfound attitude as crazy and tell you so. They do this because they are still chained. Some see the tether, know they can break it, and, out of fear, do not. Others will never admit they are chained and, to protect their mental state, must claim that you cannot be free.

This is not to say that something somewhat akin to insanity may come with this epiphany. Though, I think the insanity is more from the realization that you have been caged rather than the learning that you are free. For most, this passes, and a new equilibrium is found where you can exist and thrive - "off the list."

When you think about it, the "crazy" is staying chained to an idea - especially one that wasn't even yours, to begin with. I guess that means I have gone Middle Age Sane.

A LONG WALK IN THE WOODS

Autumn...

Leaves all but gone from the limb
no longer shield the sky
but lie slippery on the trail
not long ago, sure to the foot

In spring, the trees were so full
you could not see beyond the slightest bend
...and cared not
only patches of light danced on the ground

granted passage through pinholes in the canopy
easy now to view the valleys below
and the trail that lies ahead.
Round the bend and the creek below

brings the thought of the trailhead
and the brisk water
it makes me wish I could
have filled my canteen even more

so I could splash some on my face
and feel the coolness
that refreshes my soul
not yet winter... but the cold will come

DAN BAILEY

as surely as the next bend in the trail
and then cool water splashing my face
won't refresh… but only sting
and make me bitter for days past

But today is the day I walk.
a beautiful late fall day
leaves all but gone from the limb
me, alone with the trail
on a long walk in the woods.

DRUM BEATERS

When I was a kid, I saw a movie about a hunter in the jungle out to get his tiger trophy. Sorry, I don't remember the title. This hunter didn't actually walk through the jungle looking for the tiger. A group of natives walked through the jungle, beating drums to drive the cat toward an area where the hunter could then make his kill. The natives were lined up relatively close to each other, all beating drums and walking in unison. I am sure all the natives were individually scared of the predator cats they were chasing. However, as a group, they created enough noise with the drums to confuse the tiger, and rather than attack an unknown, the cat ran away from the noise.

There are many social situations where you see this occur as well. Sometimes in a mall or on the street, there will be a group of three or four people (yes, usually male and usually teenage or young adult) that you can hear coming from quite some distance, as if each person was talking to your Uncle Fred without his hearing aid. The "hunter" side of the male seems to have an innate knowledge of the effects of this activity, and, like an ape beats his chest, they "beat their drums" to warn others of their approach. Sometimes this is done purely to be noticed by the opposite sex. However, most of the time, I believe it occurs because the individuals within the group feel threatened in one way or another by their surroundings or immediate environment. By grouping and making more noise than necessary, the individuals can seem more significant and imposing.

Depending on their own social confidence, most of the other people in the path will acknowledge the "drum beaters" by either stepping aside, sometimes showing fear of what is coming, or by standing their ground and staring at them. People will rarely have no response to the approach of the drumbeaters. Well… maybe Uncle Fred, without his hearing aid.

I have also seen this occur in social-sexual situations, such as when two people meet and engage in a conversation that begins a mating ritual. As we see in nature shows, the male approaches the female and puffs his chest out to be noticed by her. This is "drum beating" without all the noise. The female may turn away, causing the male to work to stay in her line of sight. Still, she does what instinctive programming tells her and eventually succumbs to the "best of show" male. No, wait. That may be the mating ritual of the grouse.

Drum beating can happen in many forms and in various situations. But it almost always occurs for the same primary (or primal) reason. Whether a group or an individual, drum beating is used in an attempt to produce a larger-than-reality presence. Most drum beaters have self-esteem issues that they attempt to compensate for by puffing themselves up.

Remember, though, that people with self-esteem and other issues often act out of fear… and their fears can make them dangerous. Whether a group at the mall, your boss, or that guy at the bar.

You don't have to unmask drumbeaters, just know them

for what they are. Knowing gets you ahead of the game in the big bad jungle out there.

INTERNATIONAL DIPLOMACY

My business partner and I flew from Atlanta to New York for a business meeting one morning. One of many trips to meet with attorneys and investment bankers. Sounds exciting, doesn't it? It does have a glamour component, but the realities of these things leave a bit to be desired. I often picked up Bob at his house at 6 AM and would drop him back at 11PM the same day, just for a four-hour meeting. The rest of the time is spent getting from one traffic jam to another... whether in the air or on the ground.

This particular morning, I was in the window seat, and Bob was in the middle. (sorry - this is not a first-class experience) The aisle seat was empty, as was the one in front of it. Two Japanese businessmen came down the aisle, and one sat right behind the other. I was a little familiar with the Japanese custom of the lesser rank never putting himself ahead of or directly beside his superior, but this was the first time I had seen the practice up close and personal. The relationship was classic. The one in the front would move his body a particular way, and the other would quickly move forward and respond.

Bob had told me of his past negotiations with a Japanese camera company executive. All the executive had to do was raise a hand with fingers spread, and his "number two" would place a cigarette in his hand and light it for his superior. Not a practice you see in American business. Unless, of course, number two is a real ass-kisser (thus - "number two," I suppose).

After a while, our number two got a book and started to read. It was in Japanese, or at least it appeared to be. The characters were in vertical columns of varying lengths. My impression, origin unknown, was that the book was either poetry or, perhaps, a Buddhist prayer book. I was somewhat impressed. Here was "number two" responding to his superior; in between, he was studying and learning. Probably preparing his mind and spirit for when he would become a firm but fair - "number one."

I finally asked him what he was reading... "A devotional, perhaps?"

"No. It's a mystery... I think the gardener did it."

Well, there was nothing else to say. The picture I had drawn in my mind was still the Mona Lisa... it was just Picasso's version.

Another lesson in cross-cultural misunderstanding. No wonder we went to war. In my mind, I can see Eisenhower in a meeting with the Japanese ambassador turning to "number two" and saying, "So young man... What do you think about all this?"

"Get your paper. Read all about it. International faux pas causes World War II"

DAD

1/12/97 - I visited my father's grave. He died August 13th on a Friday (yup) 1976. So twenty years later, we finally got a stone down with his name. Don't ask me to explain why it took so long - complexities. Our family was not the type to go back to the grave much. We all thought that we had taken care of that. I went back for the first time on Father's Day 1995 when I was attempting to discover myself and maybe repair family relationships that were never whole, to begin with. After the second divorce and at 40, you are looking at things, fixing things in your life that weren't to your total satisfaction.

Anyway, I visited the grave that day in 1995. Well, I didn't actually visit the grave. I couldn't find it. Did I not remember where it was, or was the grave not marked? Or both. I walked around for a few minutes, all the while thinking I should be able to remember where my father's grave would be. I ended up just telling him that I was there and that I would check back with him later. (I assumed he wouldn't be going anywhere)

Last year my brother's wife decided it was time we did something about the marker. She went to the cemetery and talked to the folks there. Not only did we not get the gravestone, but they didn't have records of the plot for my mother (next to Dad) being paid for, and one for my sister next to that. And, they had sold my sister's to someone else. There were few alternatives. We could stack. "Bunk graves," and my sister would be next to them. Or Sis could be down one and over two - the obvious choice.

The marker was a good one. Dad was a veteran of World

War II, serving in an engineering unit that built Bailey Bridges (no relation) over rivers. As a vet, he was entitled to a free marker with military references. "No problem," they said at the cemetery. "We can install the marker for $750." "How much is your marker?" "$750, but the installation is free." Grrr. We decided to remember his military service on a perpetual care basis. So we fixed it, and the marker is there.

Funny. I still remember Dad's Social Security number, but I had his birthday wrong. For years I thought it was January 17th, but there it was on the plaque, January 10th. I said, "Hey, is that the right birthday? Isn't it the 17th?" "No, Dan, it is the 10th."

A co-worker's birthday is January 17th, and that is how I remembered it for years. OOPS.

Some people think it odd that I remember the Social Security number, but there is a reason. Dad died of emphysema. Just before Christmas of 1974, Dad came down with a bad case of pneumonia and almost died then. The doctors said he must have had the emphysema for a while and probably knew something was wrong. Anyway, he recovered from his pneumonia, but he was weakened and bedridden. Over the next year and a half, he was mostly in bed at home or in the hospital. I think I admitted him to the hospital around forty or fifty times. Each time I gave his name, his Social Security number, and his date of birth. Should I check with the hospital and see if I gave the wrong date of birth then?

I don't know when I'll visit the grave again. I only went today because I was at lunch with my mother and sister, and we were at a restaurant close to the cemetery. They asked, and I lacked a good reason not to go, so I went. My father was not someone that I picture as being a sentimentalist. That might be why I grew up with this attitude toward visiting even his gravesite. I am a touch more sentimental than he, though I deny it sometimes. I know that he is not at the grave anyway. Visiting the grave is really for the living, not for the dead.

I'll go back sometime. There is a nice view of the city skyline from the hill.

DID I DISCOVER MYSELF?

Interesting concept. Someone reading my story about going to my father's grave pointed out that I was "attempting to discover myself" and then asked if I did... discover myself. (Try to keep the questions a little simpler, would you)

I believe I did... it is a continuing process. You can't really discover all of yourself all at once. It is too much for a human to endure. Too much stuff lingering in the depths. As a principle, we all know we are imperfect. As a stark reality, the idea that everything we do could use some - a lot of - improvement is something we filter out. That way, we can ask for raises, ask that beautiful woman in the video section out for a date, and take the bigger of the last two pieces of cake at the family reunion - confident that we deserve that and more.

I was watching a nature special one night. I am trying to remember the overall theme, but I only need one part. Other animals with this ability have since been found, but they ran a spot about how the chimpanzee is the only being, other than humans, that can recognize itself in a mirror. They put a chimp in a room with a mirror, and, to begin with, this chimp thought the reflection was another chimp. Initially, she jumped back from the mirror... then started trying to get the "other" chimp to play. As part of her play, she kept moving closer to the mirror and then backed away. Since the mirror was on the floor, her foot was positioned very close to the reflection. In a moment of discovery, she noticed that the foot of the other chimp moved precisely at the same time as her own.

She looked down at the reflection of her foot and moved it - stopped - and moved it again. You could see the light go on inside her head. Then she moved her hand, simultaneously looking at the reflection and her own hand. Once the chimp was fully convinced that she was looking at herself in the mirror, she began exploring and discovering herself. She touched her nose, her ears, and her face. She opened her mouth and felt her teeth while pulling back her gums. She never took her eyes off herself for the rest of this segment of the show.

For a chimp, recognizing yourself in the mirror must be terrible. No new hairdo or tummy tuck will make much of a difference on that body. Even if the chimp recognizes a flaw, what will this little primate do about it? Thus, we get back to the difference between humans and even those animals that can recognize their own features in a mirror: Our ability to react to what we see in the mirror and make changes in our mental or physical selves if we want.

Once the chimp knew she was looking at her reflection, she carefully examined her various features... learning them through sight and touch. She moved from her foot to her ear to her nose and then her mouth. Her "discovery" didn't come all at once. What first came to her was an understanding that she had the capacity to look at herself. Through that ability, she could more fully examine each of her individual features as she desired.

Did I discover myself? Who knows? Like the chimp (hold your comments), I found that I have the capacity to look at myself. I can closely examine my individual features. I must finish looking at my "foot" before I can look at my "nose." And, being a human, I can choose to make changes, hopefully, make improvements, in the areas I identify as lacking.

In the meantime, the chimp and I are going out for a few drinks.

She does like her banana daiquiris.

FUNNY

Funny, but I had the most unusual experience recently. Actually, it isn't really that unusual, I suppose. Plenty of you have been through the same thing. You wouldn't find it as funny if you hadn't been through it. It's one of those things that isn't funny at all as you are going through it. It's only funny after you go through it and can look back on it and laugh, knowing that you have done it and don't have to do it again.

It reminds me of a story about my father. Well, not exactly what he went through, but pretty close. I remember him talking about it at the dinner table. Those were the best times. We always heard the best things about families at the dinner table. The "old days" and how things were different back then; how we would never be able to handle the "old days"; how today's kids had it so much better. Then he would tilt his head back, staring off to some distant moment, and then laugh... never even mentioning what he had just thought of.

But back to this. I am sure some people have been through the same thing and don't look back and laugh. It takes a well-adjusted person to laugh at themselves anyway. Or not really at themselves but the circumstances we find ourselves in sometimes. A few may even be offended that I would bring up such a thing. I think it would be very few, but a few nonetheless.

However, I focus on those of you who won't be offended. You have probably been through this, and look back on it and laugh. Though you may have been in a conversation and brought it up, only to have offended someone who has been through the same thing and, unfortunately, cannot look back on the experience with a smile on his or her face. This is a shame since usually, when two people who have "been there, done it, got the T-shirt and look back with a smile on their face" get together, they have a great time talking about it.

I have a friend whose family doesn't have a sense of humor about it at all. I was at his house eating dinner one night, and he brought it up. I thought his father would smack him at the table... and we were both thirty years old. His father said he had a friend who had been through the same thing and was never the same afterward. His dad said that when it changed his friend, it also changed him, and he couldn't forget it. That's why he didn't want us to talk about it.

I understood more about it that night, though my personal experience was just recently. I am glad my friend's father's experience didn't ruin my ability to look back and laugh at my circumstance. I just can't help but chuckle when I think of all I went through, dreading it beforehand and thinking nothing of it afterward. I know most of you feel the same way as I do. That is why I went ahead and wrote this. For you. Those of you that would read this and just smile. You've been there, know all about it, and look back and laugh.

SPOILER OR PARTNER

While on the phone with a friend, part of the conversation involved some of her recent business dealings. She was signing a contract with a company and was talking to the owner of that company about the agreement. She let him know that several aspects of the contract didn't protect his company very well and that she could make a few suggestions that would make the agreement much more equitable. She told me that his response to her advice was very negative and that he seemed now to be very short with her about their business dealings.

I asked her if she had considered that he had a part in writing the agreement, that he had considered its ramifications, and that he was responsible for protecting his company from harm. She caught on immediately and said, "Basically, I was telling him he was a bad businessman. Wasn't I?" Yes... you was.

I brought up a point I attempted to make in "The Santa Claus Syndrome." What was that point? People will protect their decisions and positions ardently because those decisions are Theirs. You can say what you want about your own children, but if someone else badmouths them, hang on. That person will have to see a proctologist to get whatever was close to you at the moment removed from their - well, point made. So, just like it is their baby, people think anything they have a part in creating is precious.

Sometimes, we are so experienced in a particular area and so comfortable with making/taking quick decisions/actions that we forget that others are involved. And those others may need more time, or a different delivery, to buy into what you propose.

If we need that person to help us get what we want, we must first convince them - in their way, not ours - of the need for change.

The wagon will go not faster than the slowest horse in the team.

We know we can't make headway with someone if one or both parties are in "defense" mode. If we approach an issue by telling someone they have "screwed up," they will almost surely be defensive. And, once there, they are less likely to hear anything you say, regardless of its value. We must then rethink our approach and find a way to present our information in a manner that will not inflame the other person. We must also be in tune with ourselves to recognize when we are in a defensive state.

In a previous business, I remember talking to customers that had complaints about our products and services. Occasionally, somebody would want something (usually money) for an issue over something we felt we were not responsible for. I noticed that when "my" company was being "attacked," somehow, I would go into defense mode. It was almost always on the phone, yet I could feel my body posture change. My jaw would tighten, and I would lean forward in my chair. When I recognized these physical changes in me, I understood that I was no longer thinking as a wise evaluator of the facts.

I would kindly explain to the customer that I had heard them, that I always liked to consider such issues off the phone, and that I would call them back within an hour after deliberating with myself (Stan).

As soon as I hung up the phone, I could sit back in my chair, relaxed. The only combatant present was me. I would regain a (relatively) neutral mental position and evaluate the situation from both sides. It is much easier to think of a problem from an unbiased viewpoint when you are not in "the heat of battle."

After using this method, I can't remember when I did not soften and at least met the customer halfway. And after using this method, I do not remember any time I felt that the customer was unhappy. Even if not totally happy with the decision, I thought they were pleased with how I had treated them and the thoughtful manner I had considered their request.

Kill the messenger.

When you point out someone's mistakes, they will be defensive. If you overcome the defensive position and prove them wrong, they will feel defeated. Either way, you will be seen as an opponent or spoiler. And this feeling won't just apply at the moment of your victory, but every time they see or think of you in the future. Pass them in the hall two months later, and they will have a pull in their stomach and show a frown.

Rather walk beside them and carefully lead them to their own discovery of their error and then their discovery of a different way. Then, instead of a spoiler, you will be a co-discoverer and a partner. Later, when you pass in the hall, there will be a smile and, more likely, a memory of the many things you have collaborated on since that first time you worked that problem out "together."

Most reasonable people know they are fallible in certain respects, and quite often, they know what they are doing is not working. Even in such conditions, human pride does not typically allow them to delight in accepting the responsibility for a wrong decision. Help them shoulder the weight of the mistake. Give them a way that they can maintain their pride and dignity. Even if, to you, it doesn't seem like it should be a necessity, even if they don't "deserve" it, and even if no one has ever done the same thing for you.

FUTILITY

I've grunted and groaned
And I've pissed and I've moaned
But I can't seem to get
What I want

I've tried to get focused
I've hocused and pocused
I keep saying it will
But it won't

Try as I might
There's just no end in sight
It is like beating my
head on a wall

My mind just keeps spinning
Back to the beginning
I can't seem to
Make progress at all

I turn left but not right
Like stumbling at night
When there's no one
Around to advise

With all of the trying
And all of the sighing
You'd think at the least
I would open my eyes

OBJECTIVITY AND PERSPECTIVE

Objectivity? I Object.

First off, I am skeptical that objectivity can exist. But that is just my subjective opinion. Philosophers and scientists have pondered the idea for thousands of years. Most of their answers are so twisted around, over, and under that the average person just zones out. Hopefully, I won't sound too philosophical with this, but here goes.

Objectivity requires that you first objectify something so that the resulting object can be examined. For instance, you may be selling your "home," but someone else is buying a house. The difference is that the qualities we typically refer to when we say "home" are subjective, like how comfortable you feel there and the memories you have made. A house is an object made of a mix of materials for which there is a definable cost per square foot. The home is "objectified" into a house which can then be evaluated without the emotional attachment.

You have probably heard the term "disinterested third party" regarding legal testimony, appraisals, or similar. I am sure some professionals can discipline themselves over time to offer more objective/less subjective opinions. Still, the moment someone is brought in for a consultation, they are no longer disinterested.

Lady Justice is blindfolded as a symbol of the fairness of the legal system. Either that or she is ashamed to look.

In court cases, judges recuse themselves for things like family connections, financial interests, past statements, etc. They do this to reduce the appearance of subjectivity and impropriety. We expect no impropriety, but only the appearance of subjectivity can be reduced. The actual subjectivity never goes away.

When a subject is brought to the attention of anyone, their Sensus Communis database opens and starts accessing all the data saved about that subject. As soon as that happens, someone's personal bias is involved, whether they want it to be or not.

Perspective

You are likely familiar with the effects of perspective and its influence on interpersonal and social discourse. I think a reminder, with visuals, is good for us all, as it seems that we are easily mired in an environment of rigidity with little consideration of opposing thought.

This diagram shows an overhead view of a triangular post in the middle of a circle. The R, W, and B represent the color that the outer portion of each side of the post is painted - Red, White, and Blue. The A, B, and C, and the combinations thereof, show zones of the circle sliced up based on the line of sight toward the triangular post. The geometry is simple, but this represents the complexity of human thought as it relates to perspective.

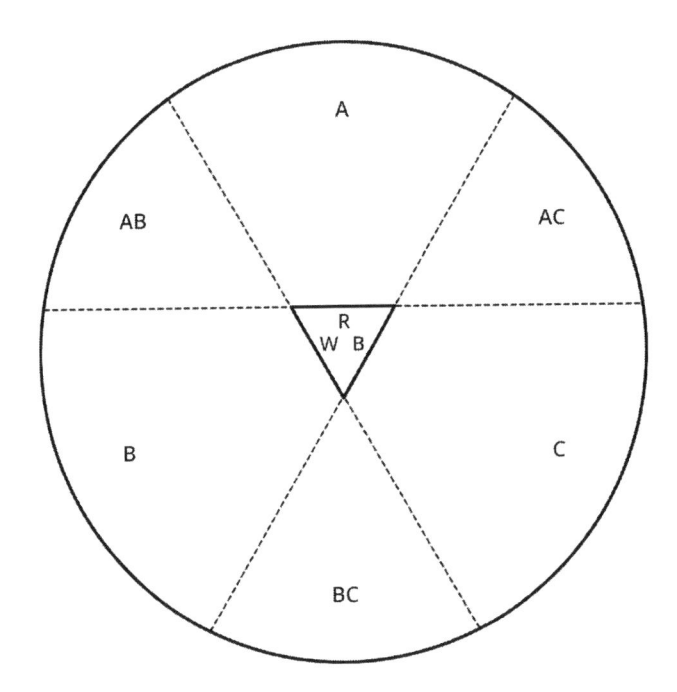

If you are facing the post and standing anywhere within the A zone, you can only see the red portion of the post. And it doesn't matter how far to the right or left, close or far, you move within the zone. The same applies to the person in the B zone, white only, and the C zone, blue only.

If you are in one of the overlap zones, you will see some combination of two colors. If you are in the center of the AB zone, then you will see an equal amount of red and white. If you move to the left (clockwise), then you will see more red and less white. If you move to the right (counter-clockwise), you will see more white than red. The pattern follows for the other overlap zones. Got it?

So, imagine one person standing where A is positioned and another standing at B. When A tells B that he is standing twelve feet from the red post, B is going to say, "What red post? The post is white." About that time, AB pipes in with, "Well, it is actually red and white." C then says, "You are all crazy. The post is blue."

Thus begins the annual family argument over Thanksgiving

dinner. If you think about it, perspective is probably the root cause of most disputes. Each of us sees things our way, and to soothe our egos, we tend to be quite protective of "our way."

In our example, it would be easy for all the parties to move around and see that the post is triangular, with each side a different color. That type of disagreement can be quickly diffused because the confusion is based on where each person is. The solution is not so easy if it is based on "what" the person is. We cannot just rewire a few million brain synapses whenever we need to consider someone else's viewpoint.

However, when we know that someone's perspective is just as real as ours, though different, and then we get ourselves to use that knowledge, we may find our lives better for it. We probably won't change our perspective, but we could increase our circle of friends and maybe, just maybe, improve the conversation at family get-togethers.

P.S. - As I write this, it occurs to me that this may be why we are so resistant to change. Most stuff isn't a flash in our minds when we talk about a familiar subject. Any subject we have an opinion on and have given much thought to will have physical connections within our brains to support the thought process. The brain uses a lot of power to wire itself and may resist change to conserve energy. Like when Bob in IT says, "It'll be hard to change. The network isn't wired that way."

SOMETHING I THOUGHT OF WHILE I WAS TAKING A SHOWER

Scientists are constantly trying to group things. They love to classify, compile, collate, and categorize. A particular interest is paid to determining the age of things. For instance, if you cannot place something in an era, age, or millennium - you are not worth your salt as a scientist. And what is the basis of this dating process? Oh, usually something like the prehensile nature of the small toe.

Based on extensive research - watching nature shows - the more a mammal could use its small toe then, the more ancient a species the sample must be. At first blush, this appears to be a solid hypothesis, but I had a cousin that could pick dandelions with his small toe, and he wasn't ancient or extinct. He was a throwback, but the family didn't talk about that much.

A popular age-determining technique is Carbon Dating. For a time, scientists said that this method was the most accurate. The problem comes because it is the "most" accurate. They don't seem to know if it is "accurate" or just the "most accurate." The second problem comes from the scientists themselves. It is common knowledge that the outcome of an experiment or test is somewhat (if not significantly) influenced by the desires or prejudices of the tester.

Say, for instance, that a scientist is a recognized specialist in the prehistoric lizards of the Someozoic Era. He finds a skeletal imprint in a rock of an unrecognized species and begins studying it. Does the subconscious desire to be known as the discoverer of a new species within his era of specialty influence the dating of the rock? Does the subconscious desire of well-meaning colleagues to pat him on the back influence their decision to concur with his findings?

What about the rock? How did the skeletal imprint get inside a rock? Not being a scientist, I cannot say with authority that the lizard did not dig his way into the middle of a rock, but it doesn't seem likely to me as a layperson. Another explanation would be that the lizard was there on a rock, minding his own business, basking in the sun when other matter, such as rock, dirt, or lava, trapped and sealed the reptile within the two layers.

My question is this. Which part of the rock do they carbon date - the chunk under the lizard or the slab above? If the lizard could have been upside-down when entombed, which is the part underneath and which was above? The rock the lizard was standing on could have been ten thousand years old, and the layer on top may be fifty-thousand. Was the lizard from ten thousand or fifty thousand years ago? Hmm...

And what if the beloved colleague that was cross-checking the dating process is a specialist in the Whichazoic Era? Would he tend to interpret the results as specific to his chosen expertise? It seems that the only solution to such a dilemma is finding someone with no specialty other than trying to figure out how old rocks are. My guess is that you would find that person... under a rock.

Easy enough to get the point. It is not enough to know someone's opinion or even how "qualified" that person is to have that opinion. To fully determine what weight to give to that opinion, you must also be aware of and understand the motivations and prejudices of the person giving the opinion. Very few people only want to know how old the "rock" is. Most want to classify and categorize the rock. Listen closely to what is said to determine motivations, and you will be closer to discovering the true meaning beyond just the words used.

Other than that - remember, I was taking a shower. Were you expecting Plato?

Note: I know science can do a lot with dating techniques. The story isn't about dating... it is about questioning.

PHOTO-SOPHIC

What truth lies within

the thousand words a picture spins?

With no contemplation of what has gone before

or what shall be

A flash and a moment is taken from time

to be seen, studied, and pondered…for

the face of a moment then becomes the subject of ages,

as if we could yet control what has passed.

Is a body one living cell?

Is the ocean one drop of water?

Yes, there is the absolute truth of the moment,

yet there is no truth since there is no whole.

But our minds will see and a thousand words then spin,

Begging, what lie does not within the truth begin?

SELF-CENTERED OR SELFISH

In an email exchange with a friend, the subject of our children came up. She wrote of her daughter, "She is looking prettier every day, but I hesitate to tell her because I stress the 'be pretty inside' stuff more than anything else."

I responded, "If I may offer an observation. I don't think you could ever do wrong in telling her how beautiful she is, inside and out. I have met many grown women who don't give themselves any credit for their beauty and are always trying to do something to change themselves or get reassurance because of that feeling. If you let a child know how beautiful a person they are, without specifying internal or external but without denying one or the other, they will grow up feeling more adequate. And, since it is only human to desire approval, they will not have to get that approval from someone else in a needy and possibly self-destructive way because they will already have it from within."

My response was well-received, as it provided a different way of looking at this aspect of parenting.

❖ ❖ ❖

But what is all this stuff about self anyway? I propose that if you aren't self-centered, you will become selfish. These two words are often considered interchangeable due to their general usage, but self-centered literally means that you center your "self."

Think of your "self" as a rosebush. If you don't weed the ground around the roots, water properly, prune, and keep bugs away, the rosebush will not flourish and may wither and die. However, take proper care of the rosebush, and you not only have roses for yourself but will also likely have roses to share with others. (don't you love metaphors?)

The "self" is very powerful. So, if you do not take care of it properly by meeting your own needs, your "self" will start looking to get its needs met in other ways. How? The alternative is to try to get that care from others through "needy" acts, which come across as you taking from others and being selfish. Unfortunately, needy acts will never fulfill the "self." They will be constantly repeated... exacerbating the "selfish" loop.

At worst, the selfish person will alienate everyone they encounter, unintentionally denying themselves their selfish ways. Selfish people need to be around other people to act out their selfishness. Conversely, self-centered people can be "self-centered" all by themselves. When you think of self-centered people in this manner, it will be no surprise that they are popular with their friends. People like spending time with people that don't want anything from them but their friendship.

Being self-centered doesn't mean that you aren't generous. If you know how to take care of your own needs, then you know when you have extra that you can share. Giving a loaf of bread is easier when you aren't starving for one.

This may seem an odd example, but it comes to mind when I think about the self-centered concept. Whenever you fly, the attendants give a safety briefing, including what to do when the oxygen masks drop out of the overhead compartment. They always say to put your mask on before trying to help your child or anyone else. Why? Because you can't help anyone else if you are unconscious. Take care of yourself first.

Self-centered... not such a bad thing after all.

THE BIG PICTURE

An intersection on a hill in the northwest suburbs of Atlanta provides a nice panorama of the city skyline on a clear day. I was stopped there at the traffic light and took in the view. As I scanned the horizon, I noticed the chimney stack for Plant Atkinson, an out-of-use coal-burning power plant just down the road from the intersection.

The height of the stack is about 200 feet tall, or thereabouts. Due to the nearness of the stack, and the effect of perspective, from that point, it appeared to be about twice the height of the Peachtree Plaza Hotel in downtown Atlanta. Of course, I know it isn't anywhere near as tall as the Plaza. A few weeks earlier, I visited the Sundial restaurant at the top of the Plaza and watched the sunset. The Sundial is at 720 feet, and the evening view is gorgeous from that vantage point. As many of you may know, the Sundial rotates, and from your seat, you can see the panorama of Atlanta and its suburbs.

As I looked at the smoke stack as it related to the Plaza, I remembered noticing the smokestack from the Plaza. Because of its height, it was easily seen from the Plaza, but only somewhat significant compared to the many other sites on the 360-degree tour of Atlanta. I thought of the difference between the two views. How, though overwhelming in size from the street, the stack was only a noticeable event from 720 feet and about 15 miles away. I thought of the "big picture" analogy that I could draw. The stack could represent something that seemed important. Yet, when put in proper perspective, viewed from 720 feet high and 15 miles away, it was only a "noticeable event."

Then I thought again, making this analogy to life. We don't live at 720 feet and 15 miles away. We live here. On the street. Where anything taller than our house is tall. We live where events in our life that are 30 feet tall, much less 200 feet, can be monumental and, sometimes, overwhelming. And, when faced with such an event - whether it be a financial, a relationship, or a family problem - the luxury of seeing it from a vantage point that renders it insignificant is all but unavailable to the average person.

Years ago, I succumbed to an acquaintance's invitation to attend a meeting about yet another multi-level marketing scheme. I only agreed because the product arena was internet access and web hosting, a business in which I was already active. A few minutes after the host had started, the upline district bigwig came breezing in. After a quick introduction, he said, "Wow. I just got from a national meeting in Columbus, and let me tell you... I am pumped!" Typical.

After a while, I asked how one would earn money by selling products. That was pooh-poohed and responded to with a review of their multi-level structure that was sure to make everyone at the table financially independent. As I pressed for an answer, he replied, "Dan. You just aren't seeing the BIG PICTURE." My response was that the BIG PICTURE is made up of small brush strokes. After getting a snarl from him, I let it go.

When facing a difficult challenge in your life, others will often say, "Look at the BIG picture. This isn't so bad." Sometimes that is good advice, and sometimes it just means that the person that said it finds your problem unimportant. When someone gives us the "big picture" line, we can often then feel less of ourselves because of our supposed narrow focus. But, sometimes in our life, we face issues that do overwhelm us. Problems that do stand in front of us like a Goliath, and we, David, without a slingshot in our hands.

TRITE

The course of a man is
not known till it's followed
The bitter of a pill
Not known till it's swallowed

Grass is still greener
Till under the feet
A fool and his money
Will never quite meet

The sun is up now
I guess I'll make hay
What kind of shoes fit
On feet made of clay?

It must be some deep
Where waters are still
I know he's gone over
I'm not sure which hill

The gift of a horse
Can't be checked for his teeth
And under a ladder
Should I walk beneath?

Is there a door-nail
That is fully expired?
Does a pin know that neatness
Is all but required?

If the church mouse yelled out

Would anyone know?
It's easy to dine
On the fruit that hangs low

I can't teach anew
A dog that's mature
Can I keep a man down
when his good is unsure?

I'm ready to reap
I guess I should sow
Is all well that ends well?
I don't really know

THE BUTTERFLY EFFECT

One of the universal points of awe among people is the feeling they get when a butterfly flies up and lands near them. The next time you are with other people when a butterfly is around, try to watch them. Mesmerized comes to mind. I don't remember being around a butterfly that every person close by did not watch intensely. We stand still... breathless... suspended... just to ensure we don't do anything that would end the moment prematurely.

One day, I was talking to my neighbor, and a butterfly landed on the sidewalk near us. Two men in their fifties stopped their conversation so they could look at a butterfly on the sidewalk. It was black with blue on the wings. I don't remember which species it was. It didn't matter. We just stared. We finally continued our conversation, but we talked as we stared at the butterfly until it eventually flew away.

Butterflies are things of immense beauty. So colorful. So mysterious. Even when they alight, the wings never really quit moving. They appear, move from flower to flower... and are shortly gone. I think that fleeting quality is what makes us take so much notice of them when they come around. The fact that we know they will only be there for a moment.

I remember catching butterflies and saving them for display. As kids, we chase them and try to snare them in nets or jars or with our hands. Put them on a board with pins through their wings so we can examine their beauty and the symmetry of their wing patterns whenever we want. School projects and science fairs typically included many a butterfly study. There was always one thing wrong with all those displays: the butterfly is nothing if not free.

Occasionally, you meet someone who reminds you of a butterfly. So beautiful... So colorful... So inspiring that you just know that you are privileged to be in their presence. They are so simple in their demeanor yet so complex in their makeup. You watch as they interact with others and move so gracefully... here and there. You know that this person, like the butterfly, has been through many stages in their life to get to this place. This place that you see now.

Shhh... Be very still.

A butterfly has landed on my shoulder.

Perhaps it will stay.

THE BUTTERFLY FACTOR

Several years ago, I had just arrived on a boat to take a cruise… one of the larger cruise ships at the time. I stood on the top deck looking down onto the pool deck, where many people congregated while waiting to cast off. I am a people watcher - no, not a stalker - and I watched as people came onto the deck, seeing what the crowd was like. You can always tell when someone is new to a cruise. They seem to be unable to look directly in front of them. Their head bounces in every direction, trying to absorb every available visual stimulation. Cruise ships are impressive that way.

I noticed four women walking together. Well, three were walking together. One was bouncing all over the place and literally jumping up and down. She was about forty years old, I would say. As I watched, I figured, of course, that this was her first cruise. A mental alert came up, though. This woman acted more like she had just been set loose from a cage and was taking full advantage of her ability to run free. Oh - she was kind of cute too. Did I mention that?

Naturally, I found my way to talk to this group. As it turned out, it was a mother and three daughters. We chatted briefly, did introductions, and went about our ways. All seemed to be lovely people. The next day we were in a port, and, purely by accident, I ran into the ladies sunning on the beach. Well, Mom was sunning on the beach. The daughters were playing in the surf, with the one daughter I mentioned still just as spirited as when I first saw them. I started a conversation with Mom and discovered that her daughter - let's call her Free Bird - had just gotten out of a tough marriage with an even tougher divorce.

Okay. Maybe, at this point, it is beginning to sound a little stalkish, but I was doing research.

Free Bird came and sat with us for a while, and we got to know each other and made plans to hang out after dinner. We went to one of the shipboard clubs for some dancing, and whenever you spend time with someone new, you learn something about others and yourself. I learned she was an aerobics instructor and was reminded I was not. Not a single slow song in the space of an hour.

Apparently, twenty-plus years ago, I could still hear in a noisy place since I do recall that we talked as we bounced. I heard more about the marriage, the divorce, and the thousand miles distance between our homes. Finally, what I heard was the voice in my mind telling me that she was a "butterfly," as I describe in the story The Butterfly Effect. A butterfly with really strong legs, but still a butterfly.

With that realization, my mind was settled. The rest of the cruise was pleasant, and I still talked with the family, but no more alone time with Free Bird.

In Butterfly Effect, I talk about humans' near-universal attraction to butterflies. I have to wonder, do we catch them in our net, or are we constantly being caught in theirs?

THE LEAF

Sometimes my thoughts drift back to my childhood when our family would go to a campground in the North Georgia mountains in the fall. The campground was next to a trout stream where we would fish. We wore knee-high waders in an attempt to keep the 50° mountain-cooled water from forcing us from the better fishing vantage points.

The foliage of the North Georgia mountains in the fall is quite spectacular. Colors abound, and even at an early age, I appreciated the show that nature provided. The trees were heavy along the creek side, and the sunlight played through the colored leaves before shimmering across the water.

As happens with mountain streams, this creek constantly alternated between a larger calm pool that came to a pile of rocks where the water roiled over and down for a few feet as it made its way to the next tranquil pool.

I remember standing in one of the calm pools, looking upstream and watching as leaves, here and there, fell to the ground and sometimes into the creek. Leaves that weren't quite dry enough, still flat and moist, would fall into the stream and almost immediately sink in, twisted by the current.

I caught a glimpse of a leaf just as it broke from the limb. This leaf was dry, curled up on the sides, and floated in a pendulum-like rhythm, back and forth as it made its way through the cool mountain air. It landed at the upper end of a pool about 20 feet long. As the leaf touched down, with its edges curled upward and stem forward like the prow of a boat, it seemed to pause, only for a moment, before being moved along the surface of the glassine pool.

Time seemed to slow as I watched the leaf make its way, turning slightly one way and then the other, down to the rocks where the fast-flowing water dropped a few inches into the pool where I was standing. The leaf made its way across a few rapids, bounced around a little, then, finding itself in the new pool, enjoyed the calm once again. I watched this leaf float past me as it dropped to the next pool, the next, and the next until it was no longer in view.

I often think of that time and how the leaf floated upon the water in the calm and tumultuous rapids. I think of myself as that leaf floating in that same pendulum-like fashion, gently touching down in the tranquil pool. I find myself floating on the surface. I am supported as I make my way on the current as it alternates between the calms and the rapids. I think of how it is only the water that becomes rapid, rocky, and tumultuous and how I merely float on the surface. I move through the varying pools as they change, conforming to whatever runs beneath.

So... When I feel the currents change around me, I often stop. And I think of the leaf.

THE SANTA CLAUS SYNDROME*

If you were raised in a home that celebrated Christmas, you probably also believed in Santa. At least you did... until you didn't. When I was a kid, for those of us who believed in Santa, there was a time in our young lives when we either got old enough or started reasoning at a level where we just couldn't believe it any longer. Many others didn't get the privilege to realize this on their own. There was always some kid named Johnny that would come to school and try to spoil it for the others. And some kid named Bobby would always fight the very notion.

"There ain't no Santa. It's just your parents sayin' that stuff to get you to eat your peas."

"Uh-Uh. No way. You're just mad because Santa knows you have cooties. Santa eats the cookies, and he brings me what I ask for. My mom and dad said he was real. The weatherman shows him on the radar."

Bobby would usually end up crying because Johnny, the little bastard, would just keep telling him that he was stupid for believing in Santa. This would give Bobby greater resolve to protect Santa from this hooligan because once people of any age have made a stand - they like to defend it. Anyway, Johnny probably grew up to open a Singing Telegram Death Notification service -

"Hi, my name is Johnny

I hope you weren't in bed

Cause I just came to tell you

That Uncle Fred is dead."

The little bastard.

We know that logic would eventually take command, and Bobby would have figured it out on his own. Ok... We hope. What happens to many adults is they never get over the need to believe in something. Sometimes blindly. Something that defies the "gravity" of logic. And I don't mean religious faith and belief in God. That is a different discussion entirely. I mean the simple day-to-day stuff. When grown adults have difficulty with, or just outright deny, acceptance of something incontrovertible, it is due to what I call the Santa Claus Syndrome.

In general, this usually happens when a person has great faith in, or an expectation of, another person. The President typically holds this place in most American citizens' minds. When President Kennedy was killed, there was a period when many people were in denial of the event. "It just can't be." We've all heard it plenty of times.

In the 90s, President Clinton came under public scrutiny for his sexual philandering.* Despite evidence of a repeated pattern of similar conduct and the fact that he lied to the country about it, Clinton's ratings were never higher than during the investigation and the resulting impeachment proceedings. Of course, the American public was ecstatic over economic prosperity. Whether or not they believed Clinton was responsible for that prosperity, nobody wanted to see any changes that would "rock the boat."

It was as if the special prosecutor was Johnny.

"Your President is a mean and nasty man that broke his promises and hasn't really done what he is supposed to."

"Uh-Uh. No way. Your just mad because... because you're Republican, and he's a Democrat. He is President, and now I have a BMW... and my 401k is appreciating... and... and I voted for him, so he can't be bad. So there."

See what I mean?

We just don't like the disappointment experienced when people in a trusted position violate that trust. Perhaps more accurately, we are more disappointed in our own judgment than in the person. Therefore, we must protect our ego by maintaining or returning that person to his or her exalted status. That disappointment in "self" is to be avoided so much that, given almost any reason we can hang our hat on, we can overlook facts - regardless of the enormity of those facts.

Another arena rife with examples is the TV evangelist. Most often, one of these guys is caught with his hand in the cookie jar (well, not actually a cookie jar, I suppose), and all it takes is a couple of tears and saying, "The devil made me do it." Six months later, he is back on TV with the admiration, devotion, and money of the people he was "ministering" to before.

I am not cynical about people, not in the least. I am, however, very realistic about them. Hell, I've disappointed myself on many occasions and have proven time and again that my feet are made of clay. The takeaway I am shooting for is that we should all at least try to understand our real reasons for a stand we take or an opinion we hold. Don't just have it today because it was what you had yesterday. Don't put so much belief in a person that if you are embarrassed by that person, you feel pressure to defend - not them - but your own judgment about them.

Santa Claus isn't real.

Just one more thing - I want a bicycle, a Roy Rogers lunch box, a choo-choo train, some Lincoln Logs, and... I want Johnny to get coal in his stocking.

*Note - you can pretty much pick your President and related circumstance to insert here

THEATER

It's all a performance
Without written line
We act for each other
Our parts to refine

There's no velvet curtain
And no closing bow
No stage left or stage right
Only - right here, right now

So speak your part wisely
Be poised yet serene
Your life will determine
How goes your next scene

SECTION V: AND THEN...

A Brief History - This is my farcical take on the development of technologies throughout our time here on Earth, with a focus on what each successive round of development seemed to give to us.

One-Liners - Whenever some interesting thought pops into my mind, usually while out with a friend or after I hit my head, I write it down in a file to contemplate, or chuckle at, sometime later.

Some of these ideas evolved into full stories and some are just stand-alone. The one-liners that follow are the stand-alone stuff, though some of these are also used in stories or elsewhere in the book.

Ok... mainly one-liners. There are some two and three-liners in there as well.

The Last Word - Well, more than one. I had to end this some way.

A BRIEF HISTORY

Long ago, pre-historic hunter-gatherers were constantly on the move, either looking for their next meal or engaged in a seasonal shift to better hunting grounds. Tens of millennia have passed, bringing what seems like an unending cycle of wars and pestilence, peace and plenty, failure and success. But at least now we can take a walk without needing to bring anything back with us. Let's take a short stroll through some of the high points of discovery and invention.

The Dawn Of Industry

With our advanced communications, we may forget there was a time when primitive man had no way of recording events. A tribal leader would ask his secretary what happened last Tuesday, and the reply would be, "I don't know!" Then primitive man learned to draw on cave walls, and we haven't stopped advancing ever since.

How it started is anyone's guess. It could be as simple as a guy named Ogg dragging his big toe in the sand. Perhaps a charred stick was scraped across a rock. Perhaps berry juice stained Ogg's hand one day, and then he rubbed the berry juice across a boulder. However it started, Ogg discovered he could draw pictures to help communicate an idea, entertain others, and make a lasting record of tribal events.

Most likely, Ogg, the tribal artist, was the less gregarious of the tribe. He was the one that watched and observed the others. As he learned more about his abilities to communicate through art, he knew that drawing in the sand had no permanence and drawing on a cave wall had no portability. Ogg needed to spend more time finding the solution to these problems. Others in the tribe probably respected his abilities or "magic." They allowed him extra time by not requiring that he hunt animals or gather fruits with the rest of the tribe... like a grant from the NEA.

Allowed the extra time in his pursuits, Ogg learned he could draw on a large leaf and make his communication portable. He could record stories on his leafy canvas or draw pictures of the animals he saw in the field. Ogg liked the portability and flexibility of the leaf, but it tended to crumble easily when it dried out. That meant he had to transcribe from the leaf onto the cave wall for later use. That was a pain, so he started experimenting with other plants and fibers.

In his spare time, another member of the tribe, Grogg, would hang out with Ogg, and he helped with the search for new material to draw on. With Grogg's help, Ogg discovered the process of making papyrus-like materials that would give the portability needed and still have some shelf life. The tribal leaders were so impressed by Ogg's invention that they sent him far away from their village to observe other areas, record his observations, and then return to let them know what was beyond their normal hunting range.

When Ogg returned, he had found new hunting grounds with fresh water and fruits. He had drawn pictures to map the way back. The leaders praised his work and moved the tribe to the area that Ogg found, and they were very successful in their new surroundings.

Grogg looked over the drawings from Ogg's trip and was taken with a picture of the sun setting... just as it touched the horizon... as if the round sun was sitting on the flat earth. That night, in a dream with possible Freudian overtones, Grogg had a vision of the picture. He saw the giant round disc seated on the planet... but this time with a hole in the middle. Something bumped into the disc, and it began to roll. The orb moved along… with the hole in the middle… as if something was in the hole and the disc was spinning around the axis.

The next morning Grogg got up, and that was the day he invented… the donut! No, wait… wrong eon.

Okay, really. The following day Grogg got up and talked to Ogg about his dream. He looked at Ogg's pictures again and studied them closely. Grogg then went out and invented the wheel. When he demonstrated it to his fellow tribesmen, the elders were amazed. As the use of the wheel grew, the tribal leaders soon realized the life of the tribe was much more manageable and wondered what else could be invented to improve the life of the tribe. With the wheel, it took fewer men to do all the work for the tribe, so they decided they wanted Grogg to devote his time to art and invention, just like Ogg. Thus was created the first research and development company - Ogg and Grogg, LLC.

Since Ogg and Grogg gave the tribe the tools to make work easier, tribal leaders were willing to let them use other men from the tribe to produce various implements. As more labor-saving devices were invented and manufactured, the work became even easier and more efficient.

After a while, one of the men making wheels for Grogg - his name was Trog - figured out a new way to make the wheels. He told Grogg about the new process, but Grogg liked his own way and would not give Trog's way a chance. Trog was convinced his way was better, so he left Ogg and Grogg to form a start-up business called Trog & Associates. Trog was working alone but thought "& Associates" would make his company sound bigger.

The tribal leaders were worried that time was being wasted by having Grogg and Trog make wheels, so they appointed one of the younger leaders, Brog, to pay close attention to what each of them was doing. After a moon, Brog reported back to the leaders. As it turned out, Trog's way was better than Grogg's, and soon the tribal leaders reassigned the men from Grogg's wheel-making to Trog's group. Brog was the first efficiency consultant.

It wasn't so bad for Grogg. Ogg had some new designs for spears made of a heavy, shiny rock he had found and decided to call iron. Grogg started manufacturing spear tips, and they revolutionized the hunting process.

With each of Ogg and Grogg's new inventions, the tribe gained efficiencies that allowed more tribesmen to devote themselves to manufacturing... creating yet still more efficiencies... and so on.

Something else also happened due to the shift from all the men having to hunt. For as long as anyone could remember, all the men had to wear darker animal skins, providing camouflage while hunting in the forest. Since the men of Ogg & Grogg and Trog & Associates didn't have to hunt, they could use light-colored animal skins for clothing. Another first: The dawn of white animal-skin jobs (there were no collars back then).

Nature & Technologies

Nearly all industrial and technological creations mimic what the human body and mind have always done at one level or another or, in some cases, what has been observed in nature. I use the term "All" very freely here. I should qualify by saying that I haven't had time to think of everything... but for everything I have thought of, I have found a comparison to a human or natural capability or trait.

It started with Ogg and Grogg. You can hit things pretty hard with your hand, but the harder you hit, the more your hand hurts. Long before Ogg learned he could draw with berry juice, he picked up a tree limb about the same time Grogg walked up behind him and startled him. Out of reflex, Ogg spun around quickly - limb in hand - and knocked Grogg out cold. Ogg smiled, knowing that the last time he hit someone that hard, his hand hurt for days. Since Grogg was an affable type, he wasn't mad at Ogg and was intrigued by Ogg's use of the stick to do what would usually be done with a hand. While experimenting with their newfound tool, they noticed they could swing the stick much faster than their hand because of its length. The quicker they wielded the stick, the harder they hit an object. With a bit of practice and the right stick, they improved their drives by as much as fifty yards.

One of the most simple tools man has ever devised is the lever. The lever uses three points: 1) where the lever is fixed or pivots from, 2) where force is applied to the lever, and 3) where force is expended. The lower arm is a lever device. The elbow is the fixed/pivot point. The muscle is attached below the elbow and is how force is applied to the lever, and the hand is where force is expended. I doubt if the first person to use a lever, probably pre-human, noticed the similarity with arm function. Still, there was likely an innate recognition that they were, in effect, extending their body.

How about Grogg's wheel? Glad you asked. Think about it. A wheel is a round object with a continuous surface that rolls across the ground. Now, picture in your mind a woman walking (I prefer to imagine women rather than men)... and she is wearing flats - no heels. Her foot raises and moves forward. As her foot starts to move downward, the bottom of the foot approaches the ground at an angle, causing the heel to touch first. As the step continues, the bottom of the foot comes in contact with the ground, gradually, from the back of the heel to the front of the foot. Then at the end of the step motion, the bottom of the foot gradually disconnects from the ground from the heel to the toe. It is as if the foot is just one small section of the circumference of a wheel coming into and out of contact in a circular motion. This example is reinforced by thinking of a wagon wheel hub with spokes and no outer rim. Mentally, visualize putting shoes on each spoke and rolling the wheel. The shoes contact and break contact with the ground in much the same manner as a walking foot. Can you see that?

In the 1500s, Leonardo da Vinci envisioned and drew a rough sketch of a helicopter-like flying vehicle and a wing mechanism for a flying machine. Every sighted person that had ever lived on the planet had seen a fish swim underwater or watched a bird fly and likely wondered if they could do the same. Leonardo had a pen, paper, and a gift for describing his ideas in words and drawings.

The gift that da Vinci had was also a problem for him. Despite his ability to think and envision well beyond the norm in the 1500s, for many of his ideas, the underlying technology to create these machines did not exist. He could only conceive how to turn his helicopter's rotor or flap his flying machine's wings with manpower and gears. Since the only construction materials he knew of were the available metals and wood, it was easy to see a man couldn't provide enough power to lift the device's weight. Stay tuned for the Wright Brothers.

In some of my reading about da Vinci, it has been mentioned that he had worked on a design for a submarine but didn't promote or develop it because he knew it would be used in the furtherance of war. Kind of odd since he made so many other war machines, so the concept of a navy with a submarine must have really scared him. In the mid-1800s, industrial technologies had matured, and semi-submerged boats such as the Monitor and the Merrimac had been built. Then, Jules Verne wrote a book about an ocean-going submarine... something that had not been created except in the imagination. What da Vinci and Verne wrote about, someone else engineered. Many failed at the task, and the first viable, modern submarine was finally produced just at the turn of the twentieth century.

More than just thought had changed over the three hundred and fifty years since da Vinci. It wasn't that the human mind could not imagine such things; the human experience had not advanced to the physical creation of those mental images. The ability to create steel in reasonable quantity and consistent quality did not occur until the 1800s, and the internal combustion engine was not invented until the late 1800s. It took the combination of these two major technological breakthroughs and many others to make three hundred fifty years of thought a reality. This is likely why the airplane and the submarine were made viable nearly simultaneously.

Like the lever and the wheel, planes and submarines were technological extensions of natural occurrences. Eventually, somebody was going to figure it out.

Today, we have TV, audio recording, telephones, and computers. To the average person, technology is a beautiful thing to which they never have to give much thought. You don't have to understand how TV actors and sets become electrons and how the electrons travel through the air and miraculously appear on your TV screen for your viewing pleasure. Thankfully. The fact is that a great deal of technology is involved in delivering TV to you. The cumulative knowledge about photography, sound waves, electricity, radio frequency transmission, and dozens of other subsets of technology had to come together to create TV.

But what is TV? (besides a reason for playing with a remote) You can go to a play and watch actors perform, hear their lines spoken, and have the same thing. You then have the memory that you can "watch" repeatedly in your mind. TV is just a method for "picking up" the play and bringing it to you rather than you going to it.

In broad terms, TVs, computers, and cell phones merely copy what humans do daily, though usually faster and over much greater distances.

Computer networks mimic society. One person alone can do things. Two working together can get even more done. Get four or five people working together, and you can get a lot done... and start a boy band. One computer sitting alone can make a person more productive. A computer on a local area network allows for greater productivity and centralized storage, which provides greater efficiency. Attach that network to the Internet, and, well, you know what that does. Still, all our technology is merely reproducing what is done naturally, though again, over more considerable distances and speeds.

Technology Acceleration

Like da Vinci, true innovators can think past several layers of technological advances. Some scientist did that when it was conceived that living things are made up of cells or that a molecule is the smallest particle of matter long before there was a microscope to confirm any of that. Eventually, the practical caught up with the theoretical, and the first microscope revealed a bunch of squiggly little things that are just about everywhere.

Each new technology adds to knowledge, giving birth to more theoretical and, then, more practical knowledge. The ancient Greeks had offered the concept of atoms, which, to them, meant indivisible. Likely, they had yet to conceive of the structures we call an atom or molecule. Their theory was probably more along the line that big stuff is made of a lot of small stuff. By the time I got to school, we were taught that atoms are made up of particles called protons, neutrons, and electrons. Current particle theory is at the quark-muon-boson stage... I think. I am sure someone is waiting in the wings, formulating thoughts, about to crank up the Large Hadron Collider and postulate the next level of "trust me, this is as small as it gets."

In the early 1800s, we had electricity, and by the mid-1800s, Samuel Morse had created the first telegraph device. By 1876 Bell had invented the telephone. Marconi gave us wireless communication at the cusp of the twentieth century. Born from this trifecta of invention, an innumerable amount of people have built upon the successes of their predecessors to get us where we are today and where we will be tomorrow.

In the process of Technology Acceleration, each technological advance creates efficiencies that either speed up the process of creating the next technological advance or free up more people to apply themselves to creating even more technological advancements. One person invented the wheel, making life easier for the rest. Maybe, as in Grogg's story, one or two more people had free time because the wheel had made everyone more efficient. They used that free time to think of other inventions and technologies. Each advance in industry and technology spawned further thought toward the next level of technology. It was as if at each level, some person, or perhaps several, would look closely at the new technology and say to themselves, "Hey, if we can do that, then we can probably also do this!"

Okay. I assume the wheel was invented by one person. In the early course of history and throughout the industrial age, with a few exceptions, we see that the most notable advances were the brainchild of a person working alone. Granted, Alexander Graham Bell's assistant was on the other end of the line when the call sounded. Still, he got very little credit and probably even less money. As the phone and other technology and communication enterprises grew and sprouted other enterprises, money and talent became concentrated in fewer and fewer companies and institutions.

Especially across the 1950s, 60s, and 70s, it seemed like all the brilliant people were at some vast, big-money corporation or government lab. In actuality, it wasn't "all" the smart people. The rest of the intelligent people were busy doing other things. Fifty-something years ago, large and powerful entities were the only places that had the money, infrastructure, equipment, and time to allow for innovation. And, due to the limitation of resources, only the cream of the collegiate cream graced the halls. The rest of the brilliant people were busy working and raising a family. If there was a chalkboard at home, it likely displayed scribbled messages about ball games and eggs, not world-changing formulae left for hours, days, and weeks of contemplation.

When computing power was put into the hands of the average

man, it allowed him or her to transfer knowledge and ideas to a device that can reflect back with an ability to refine that knowledge and improve upon it. This created a personal Technology Acceleration. The technology arena drastically changed once the masses became equipped with PCs. Instead of almost all the innovation coming out of corporate brain trusts, nearly anyone who applies their imagination can dream up the next world-changing widget.

I use the words "imagination" and "dream up" very deliberately, as there are clearly people that excel in the "what ifs?" of life. Technology Acceleration has not only given those people more time to contemplate innovation, but it has also provided phenomenal personal tools to assist them. In some ways, we have circled back to the days when the power of the individual as the driver of innovation is quite strong.

That said, we are moving into the era of artificial intelligence and on the horizon of a time when robotics will fully find its way out of the manufacturing floor and onto the kitchen floor. I believe robotics and AI will cause the pendulum to swing back toward corporate and government control of innovation in the coming years because of the required capital and infrastructure. I don't know if I excel at "what ifs," but I do wonder if this will be the last swing of that pendulum.

As we have "multiplied and subdued the earth," we have developed technologies that I believe place us on a trajectory toward future lives that will see all of our needs met with a flicker of thought, an instantaneous response of AI, and the whir of a molecular level 3D printer.

It does make me wonder, though. When all our dreams come true... what will we then dream of.

ONE-LINERS

Daily Life

Whenever he puts his best foot forward, I wonder if he is about to trip someone.

Are you still responsible for your actions if your alter-ego has stolen your identity?

I have been walking so much that my smart watch reported itself as stolen.

Every time the computer boots up and little windows pop up and quickly disappear, I think to myself, "What government agency have I pissed off now?"

If I kind of like the rut I am in… can I call it a groove?

I don't need it to go back in place so much as I need it to go back in time.

Yes, I sometimes talk to myself. It seems to help. Not sure why I talk to myself in a British accent, though.

When you are wrong, be the first to admit it. It takes all the fun out of your mistake for everyone else.

I just finished my first day as a grape processor at a winery. I crushed it.

You know you've done a lot of online shopping when you are tired of popping bubble wrap.

You aren't really a failure unless you quit trying. Until then, you just suck at what you do.

Whenever I hear, "Leaves little to the imagination", I think, "You just don't know my imagination."

"And, you are the responsible party?" To which I replied, "Party. Yes. Responsible. No."

I don't mind being shocked, but I don't like to be surprised.

I was at the dermatologist and was flattered when she said she likes a man with a bald head. Then I realized I was just easier to examine.

I have slowed down so much that it is still yesterday for me.

This Halloween I am dressing up as a ghost of my former self.

Even my other personalities are tired of putting up with me.

Are part-time comedians part of the giggle economy?

Apparently, I have been spending too much time playing this computer game. I just reached a new level called Intervention Recommended.

Phone solicitor: you can earn an additional 500 points if you listen to this exciting new offer.
Me: I don't think I can handle the excitement.

This software has a new button called "Dictate." I press it, but people still don't do my bidding.

When spending time with someone, you always gain something, even if it is a new-found appreciation for finding other people to spend time with.

As they discharged me from the hospital, they gave me a long list of things that I won't do.

Science (Ish)

During the discussion, Edison got so direct that Tesla had to try an alternate course of action.

Two metric weights side by side are called parallelo"grams."

Two carbon molecules were sitting drunk in a bar, contemplating the meaning of half-life.

If two people are riding parallel on a carousel, then they are going straight to nowhere.

It occurred to me that medieval bell ringers were probably glad they didn't use military time,

At The Bar

There is a reason that Somber and Sober are only one letter apart.

Have another drink. It will improve your opinion of me.

Do you believe life begins at a) birth, b) conception, or c) the third shot of tequila?

Quick! Let's plan something before the mature part of my brain wakes up.

I said I would pay attention… not your bar tab.

Would a swim-up bar automatically be considered a "dive"?

Two Old Guys Are Sitting In A Bar:

As the cute bartender walked away:
1 - "She called me 'babe'!"
2 - "As she gently wiped the applesauce from your chin."

Getting ready to leave the bar:
1 - "We're going to have to pay for this."
2 - "Today and tomorrow."

As a regular leaves the bar:
1 - "She never did anything for me."
2 - "Me either. I asked and asked, but nothing."

After discussing the multiverse theory:
1 - "So, in some universe, that 25-year-old will go home with me."
2 - "That would be the looney-verse.

Puns

What did the ketones say to the urethra? "We come in pees."

That giddy feeling you have when you do something delightfully wrong... it comes from sin-dorphins.

The woman that had the most children was "fecund to none."

What large river animal can help you quit smoking and other bad habits? A hypno-pottamus.

What do you call twins that go crazy? Hystereo.

When should the giant French wave arrive? Tsun ami.

Relationships

I was with her when she dumped her boyfriend... he barely made a splash.

I had the name of an ex tattooed just below my ankle. As

relationships go, she was just a footnote.

I have decided to go and embarrass myself on my own rather than have you along to help.

A female friend asked why men always look at younger women: "Am I supposed to appreciate the Mona Lisa because she is 500 years old or because she is beautiful?"

I always knew where she stood because it left shoe prints on my back.

It seems that everything is better when it is fried. Which, for some reason, made me think about my in-laws.

We were like brothers... he was Cain, and I was Abel

Hate is often nothing more than love without hope.

Dating a married person - if you are going to bite into that apple, don't be surprised if you bite into a worm.

Like the rails of a track, we were kept apart by the same things that tied us together.

I guess that regardless of what you are looking for, if you are looking for something *in particular*, then it is hard to find.

In your early twenties, you fight over who is going to sleep in the "wet spot". After you have been married for twenty years... you fight over the fact that there just don't seem to be any wet spots anymore. Once you get into your later years, arguments about sleeping in the wet spot usually end up involving the words "adult diaper."

So much can be learned from seeing someone just for a moment... the way they move through a crowd, the way they interact with people and things.

Advice

Never put a stamp on an envelope until you have already written the address on it.

Never tell a woman there is a spider on her shoulder till you have already knocked it off.

Shyness is something for which the world does not have much patience.

Don't throw the apple with the worm away unless you have plenty without worms.

Insist on treating yourself well, and others will follow your example.

Never give anyone a piece of your mind unless you are sure you'll have enough left for yourself.

Rather than ask for the time, ask for the watch. You never know.

The "yard" of life has a lot of dogs running around in it. Watch where you step. and you won't have to clean your shoes quite so often.

Instead of trying to change for those around you… change those you are around.

The past is a nice place to visit but you wouldn't want to live there.

The Truth Of The Matter

An extensive vocabulary is best used for listening.

The only time life can bite you in the ass… is when you aren't facing it!

Whenever you hear someone say something like, "Well, what

would be ideal..." Remember that Ideal = "I" + "deal" and what you hear after that word is almost always a statement of what that person wants out of a situation, often without consideration for the "you-deal."

Honesty is not the presence of perfection, but the absence of deception.

It does seem that we learn the most when the class is hardest... not when it is easy.

It is a small war indeed that can be won with a single battle.

The older you get, the younger "old" looks.

We all have different ways of *not* seeing things.

No one can atone for something that they didn't do.

The most valuable "yes" comes from someone that has the option of saying "no."

Everything higher in the food chain feeds on what is below. But, upon death, everything lower in the chain gets its revenge.

Often, the shell of beauty will collapse from the vacuum of an empty soul.

Before the fact, it's a bribe, after the fact, it is a gratuity.

Getting off to a good start is not a finish.

The velocity of animosity determines the ferocity.

The flower is for a moment, but the seed goes on and on.

Everyone believes that **they** are the ones standing outside Plato's cave.

Like a finely cut diamond, each person has facets that can only be seen when examined from various angles.

Nothing can be divined except for that which has already

occurred.

Now that I am back to normal, nothing's changed.

It is easy to pass a rule for everyone. It is harder to enforce it on a particular person.

I am both the clay... and the hands that shape.

There's not much use for a rule that is never broken.

It isn't the way you screw up that counts... it's the way you recover.

The more you explain it, the less you believe it.

Which do you fear most... Things changing or things staying the same?

It is a *newly lit* candle that can be extinguished by a mild breeze.

We frustrate ourselves the most when we do not do what we should have done *when* we should have done it.

You don't have to balance every time... balance often comes over time.

Life is a journey that ends before you get to where you are going.

THE LAST WORD

Thank you so much for reading my book. I hope it has entertained, enlightened, or both. If it left you confused… welcome to my world!

In the story McMansions, I mentioned being the designated driver for some female friends. Not mentioned in the story was that one of the ladies sitting in the back seat was wearing that spray-on glitter… as I found out when cleaning my car afterward. And a year later. And a year later. It just wouldn't go away. On the plus side, each time I saw it, it was a pleasant reminder of a great time that I had.

In the sappiest of metaphors, I hope that, like that glitter, some of my stories stick with you and provide you with a pleasant reminder of our time together.

I am sure that Stan will have more stories and thoughts to be shared down the road.

Made in the USA
Columbia, SC
21 August 2023